# TIES AND T-SHIRTS

Bridging the Communication Gap in
America's New Workforce

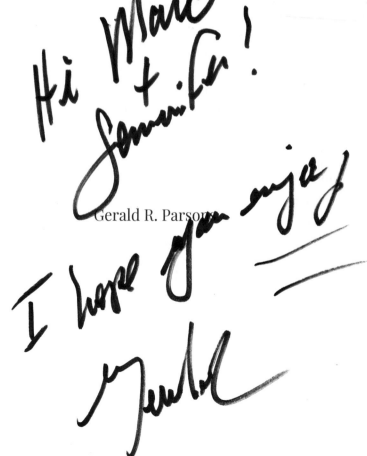

Hi Marc
+
Jennifer!

Gerald R. Parsons

I hope you enjoy

Gerald

**Ties and T-Shirts: Bridging the Communication Gap in America's New Workforce**

Printed in the United States of America.

First Printing, 2020

For permission requests to use the materials in this book please contact:

Gerald Parsons
Life Languages International
2711 Valley View Lane
Suite 103
Dallas, TX 75234

gerald@lifelanguages.com

www.lifelanguages.com

# Endorsements

"An astonishing breakthrough book that teaches the real fundamentals of bridging communication across a multi-generational workforce. A must read for every company's HR, OD, training, and learning and development leader."

Ginny Gray, Ph.D.
Organizational Psychologist
Talent Management/Organizational Development

"In today's dynamic, ever-changing culture, very few companies will thrive without the support of an effective internal communication system. In his new book, "Ties and T-Shirts...Bridging the communication gap in America's new workforce", Gerald Parsons provides an absolutely detailed and comprehensive look at communication matters that occur within most companies. Information is this enlightening book introduces us to a unique analysis of the multi-dimensional factors that impact and influence an organization's communication system and provides strategic insights for maximizing the efficiency and effectiveness of such systems.

The author provides an exemplary discussion that shows the reader exactly how to bridge the gap between multi-generational employees through the use of a number of excellent strategies, including analyzing and understanding the unique communication styles and behavioral characteristics of individuals through the 7 Life Languages™. This insightful information will have a profoundly positive impact on helping to create a productive and collaborative work environment in any organization. I whole-heartedly recommend this book to employees and managers at all levels within any firm. Tremendous understanding, knowledge, and wisdom will definitely be gained from reading it."

Linda Morable, Ph.D.
Management Professor,
Richland Campus, Dallas College

"A must-read for today's leaders. Your organization needs every-one to communicate well. By applying the Communication IQ™ methods, and being mindful of generational differences, you can learn how to get better performance from your team."

Rich Russo, CEO
Build Connect LLC

"Gerald Parsons has written a must-read primer for anyone seek-ing better communication and productivity within a diverse work-force. The book is loaded with value-driven insights and practical tips that can be easily be implemented for lasting results. Read this book - and learn from one of the best."

Dr. Brandon Honeycutt
Co-Founder, Livingfluent.com

"As both an employee of small and large businesses – and espe-cially as a business owner working with small business owners – I have experienced the challenges of management and leadership. Almost 100% of the problems I've seen come from poor com-munication. There is a lack of understanding that a person can adjust his or her communication style. Most team members will run through fire for a leader they respect. And all leaders will go to the mat for a team member they appreciate. As our work environment grows from the more Traditional style to adding Millennials and beyond, those of us that might be more Traditional, Baby Boomer or GenXers need to be able to adapt to the changing workplace communications. And the younger generations need to have a better understanding of how to get their ideas clearly communicated and truly heard. This book is a must-read for leaders, but a gem for upcoming managers and employees. Once we all get past the communication challenges, it opens up a straight path to workplace loyalty and business success."

Susan Fennema
Chaos Eradicating Officer (CEO)
Beyond the Chaos

"Ties & T-Shirts provides a refreshing and evidence-based approach to solving generational workforce challenges. There are many books on the market that describe the generational difference in the workforce. Most books on this topic focus on instructing employers on what they need to do to adapt to the needs of the latest generation entering the workforce. While understanding these needs is important, this single-focus approach does not consider the existing workforce that they are entering. Failing to take a holistic view of your workforce generational differences and needs will result in unhealthy relationships and a dysfunctional workforce, as this book accurately points out, effective communication is the foundation to strong working relationships that enable organizations to be financially successful. The importance of healthy organizational communication can be likened to the difference between growing a garden in good soil and growing a garden in bad soil. Good communication is the good soil that produces fruit such as collaboration, accountability, initiative, and innovation. I highly recommend Ties & T-Shirts to every leader who wants to better understand how to honor and leverage the generational differences in their workforce to accelerate individual and organizational success."

Leslie Horwitz MBA, M.Ed. SPHR-SCP
Vice President, Talent & Organizational Development
Fortune 500 Insurance Company

"I met Gerald Parsons though our Managing Partner Leadership Advisory Danielle Mairs. I knew he had to be special because Danielle is not easily impressed and doesn't suffer fools well. I was somewhat skeptical as I've evaluated hundreds of psychometric products over a forty year career in human capital consulting. Before meeting Gerald, I took his Life Languages™ assessment. To my utter amazement, it nailed my communications style better than any instrument I've ever seen, and it took less than twenty minutes to take. The accuracy and efficacy of Gerald's assessment got my attention and compelled me to have subsequent conversations with him.

After several conversations and a bunch of due diligence, I've determined that Gerald and his outfit are the real deal. Beyond having great assessment products, Gerald practices an approach that resonates with me like few do. He speaks of making relationship deposits even when the end game is not clear. He speaks of being willing to work on relationships that seem worthwhile, even when there is no clear evidence of impending success. The concept of never burning a bridge unnecessarily is one we could certainly use in Washington D.C. today!

Gerald's work around communications is world-class. It has been my experience that far too many leadership teams will never reach their full potential because they are either unwilling to foster, as

Gerald says, the three C's – **Connection, Communication** and **Collaboration**. Beyond being willing, leaders have to know how. Gerald's work is all about helping individuals and team communicate intentionally and effectively, while recognizing and appreciating different styles and preferences. I highly recommend Gerald's organization, consulting model and this book!"

Rob Andrews
Chairman and CEO
Allen Austin

"I'm a big fan of Life Languages. After completing the assessment, I not only better understood my communication style, I could also learn to adapt to other people's preferred styles. I hear over and over how communication is the most important challenge most businesses face. Life Languages can dramatically improve that challenge faced by most businesses."

Tom Bronson
Founder & CEO
Mastery Partners

"Seeking wisdom, pursuing knowledge and applying the two with understanding has always proven the best solution for any troubling situation for this Influencer. But, as our company grew, I found myself falling short understanding how to bridge the generational gap with my employees who are also my children. T-shirts & Ties came at the time I needed it most. I found the wisdom, knowledge and the applications of understanding to be effective. I'm looking forward to our team being better equipped to grow our company, effectively... together. I now have tools to rest in our past success strategies while embracing the ideas of the next generation, which is creating an environment for all of us to be a part of our future successes."

Mary Fontenot
Managing Agent / Owner
Agape Benefit Specialists LLC
dba Fontenot's Insurance Agency

# Founder's Message

FRED AND ANNA KENDALL

Founders: Life Languages International, LLC™

Developers: Kendall Life Languages Profile™ and Communication IQ™ Assessment

Authors: *Communication IQ* and *Speaking of Love*

Is the world becoming more confusing each day? That seems to be the message from a multitude of voices. And it appeared to be especially true in the corporate world. New and old attitudes, methods, work styles, as well as relationships often collide and clash, leaving each person *"wondering what is happening and where do I go from here"?*

This book has answers that will help you successfully navigate the corporate waters, during both the calm and turbulent seasons. Whether you are just starting in your career or have reached the pinnacle, we are confident the information in *Ties and T-shirts* will insure smoother sailing.

*Ties and T-shirts* will also help you recognize your value, position and significance in the corporate world of today. You will discover that you have within you, innate and unique gifts and intelligences that will more clearly define how you understand yourself and others,

We are delighted to recommend this book by Gerald Parsons, who has been a longtime friend and is the CEO of our corporation, Life Languages International, LLC™, established in 1993. Gerald has proven to be a successful leader, a builder of people, and a man of great character, who inspires character in others. He is well qualified to develop and prepare leaders for the challenges in today's world.

Enjoy reading *Ties and T-Shirts* and speaking the languages of success!

# Dedication

In my life I have dedicated many things and have been dedicated to many things. For instance, I am dedicated to good Cajun food and college football (Purple and Gold).

But, when it comes to the appreciation of people, I am humbled by the faithfulness of a few folks that have made a commitment to walk out my journey beside me, mentor me, give unselfishly to me, invest in my dreams, give me the gift of correction, and extend unconditional love.

If a man or woman has just a few of these relationships in a lifetime, they are truly wealthy. So, I am dedicating this book along with all my stuff to these people.

My wife, Sharon Parsons, whose been married to me for 42 years. (This woman is a saint.) In each of those over 15,000 days, she is an example of grace and love. You are the love of my life and I am a blessed man.

My family, Joel and Hannah Ashton, Ryder, Maddox and Brodie Randon and Lindsay, Kennedy and Randy. Each of my children and grandchildren have brought me immense delight as I enjoy first place in the grandparent competition, at least, in my mind.

My mentors, Fred and Anna Kendall, the founders of Life Languages™. Both have been great counselors who have taught both my family and I the real meaning of character, integrity and forgiveness. As you read this book, you will notice some of my personal core values sprinkled throughout the chapters. In no small part, the Kendalls helped me to shape those values.

There would be no opportunity to share this book, our company, or the Communication IQ™ tool and methodology with so many of you without the tireless dedication of our executive team and major contributors.

- Allison Hendrickson, Chief Operating Officer US

- Chris Walker, Chief Information Officer

- Paul Nedoszytko, President CIQ™ Ltd UK

- Jenni-Sanford Nedoszytko, VP CIQ™ Ltd UK

- Carolyn Santos, Master Coach Emeritas

- Rich Russo, VP Corporate Development US

- Dr. Ginny Grey, PhD. I/O Psychologist Org Mgmt US

- Jimmy Curtin, VP Sales US

This leadership team is amazing, insightful, powerful and delightful. Thank you!

# Table of Contents

# Introduction

There are approximately seven billion people in the world today. Each one of them is important, unique, and valuable. Many have limitations and opportunities that are different.

Even though this book is written to address a need I perceive to be critical in our nation, the deep need of every human is to be heard and understood. From a hungry baby crying in the poorest of countries to the CEOs of Fortune 500 companies, this need is not limited by ethnicity, status, wealth, education, gender, or age.

I believe in this so much that we founded this company on this one principle. At the end of this book there is a link that will take you to a place where you can register as a donor at my expense from the proceeds of your purchase. We will donate 10% of all proceeds from the sale of this book for you to United Rescue Alliance (www.unitedrescuealliance.org), an international non-profit organization dedicated to helping those who fall victim to natural disasters.

You may think this isn't much, but it doesn't take much to make a difference.

Communication today is more critical than ever before. Never in my lifetime (I'm a baby boomer) have I ever experienced a more careless and reckless disregard for humanity and individual character than in the way communication is delivered today. It is used to destroy, discourage and conceal instead of to create, inspire and reveal.

As always, between generations, the struggle is real to communicate effectively, and many times, we figure it out after great damage to trust has been done and any relationship equity that may have been on deposit has been bankrupt.

In this book, my purpose is to provide the materials – inspiration and information – to generations divided by communication gaps at every level simply because we all desire to be heard and understood.

I hope you can use this book and our Communication IQ™ system to make your relationships stronger, your companies more effective and your families more loving.

So find a quiet place, listen to this book and use it as my deposit into our relationship equity.

# CHAPTER 1

---

# It's Predictable ... Millennial Miscommunication

The workplace of today looks absolutely nothing like it did just a decade ago. The reason? – Diversity.

When I say diversity here, I am not referring to cultural diversity, but to the demographic and generational diversity that we see in many of our offices today. Walk into almost any office and you will find at least three of the five generations of employees – Traditionalists, Baby Boomers, Generation X, Millennials and Generation Z. (And in a matter of years, we will have an update to this book to include Generation Alpha – who are being referred to as the "glass generation" – and their children, Generation Beta.)

The harsh reality of today's workforce is that it is too diverse to have a "one size fits all" style of management. However, the good news is that it can be understood by categorizing the different types of employees and knowing their working styles, personalities, temperaments, and other human elements that make them unique.

## A Brief History

Let's begin with the oldest members of the workforces – the Traditionalists. Born before 1946, the traditionalists are, as the name suggests, quite orthodox in their approach towards managing teams and running organizations. These are the kind of employees who have started their careers in the same company and do not intend to go elsewhere. Fiercely loyal, they may hold strong notions and expect to be treated as more senior by virtue of their age and their longevity within an organization. The main drivers or motivators for this generation of employees are respect, recognition, stability and ensuring that their work benefits the company in the long run.

Next are the Baby Boomers, who would typically be categorized as those born between the years of 1946 and 1964. Baby boomers are called so since these were the years when there was a massive increase in the birth rate following World War II, as the country aimed to find its footing once again. Employees belonging to this generation are very optimistic, competitive workaholics who typically live by the mantra "teamwork makes the dream work." More often than not, they put duty above all else and are keen to mentor younger members of the team.

Then there is the generation that arose in the wake of the dot-com bubble – Gen X. This is the generation that is primarily focused on having work-life balance and wanting more from their jobs than salaries and health benefits. They seek to be valued and heard within their companies and are quick to move to a place where they can find these human-centric perks. They are the first generation of employees who broke the 9-5 workday cycle and introduced flexible work arrangements in many companies.

Now comes the generation that actually forms the majority of the modern workforce – Millennials. Often touted as lazy, bohemian in taste and disloyal, this generation is primarily responsible for completely transforming the workplace as we knew it. Extremely competitive and tech-savvy, millennials put their unrelenting adaptability to great use by making sure their companies are always ahead of the curve and following the latest and best trends.

Millennials tend to value open communication, acceptance of new, trendy, or even risky ideas, and mutual understanding that work must add value, not just fill time. Additionally, millennials prefer to work for employers who believe in helping people over helping institutions. For the millennial employee, it is far more compelling to work for something that is tied to a higher purpose or mission than to simply reach departmental numbers or organizational goals.

The last, and newest generation is Gen Z – the generation that made the term "glocal," in which organizations are characterized by local and global structures, the new normal. Extremely entrepreneurial and creative, this generation has most recently started stepping into workplaces and often looks for guidance and mentorship from their supervising millennials. Gen Z values salary far less than any of the previous generations and desire to put a spotlight on issues that are very close to their heart such as climate change, sustainability, and global hunger to name a few. Gen Z tend not to separate professional and personal beliefs and hold strongly to a unified view of everything in the world.

19

There is no denying that today's employees want much more than nice perks, free lunches, and a fat bonus check at the end of the year. Employees today – especially millennials – desire for their bosses and the companies to whom they dedicate 40 hours or more a week, to foster honest and authentic communication with them.

A survey conducted in 2015 by 15Five found that out of 1000 full-time employees across the United States, 81 percent of them desire to join a company with "open communication" as one of their core values. This is far above health benefits, gym subscriptions, and free lunches every Friday. For millennials, the percentage is slightly higher with 84 percent saying an open communication policy was more important than any perks.

The Deloitte Millennial Survey predicts that by 2025, millennials will constitute 75 percent of the global workforce. As millennials already constitute the majority of the workforce and are set to take up leadership roles with their incoming Gen Z counterparts, it is important to understand some key factors that would impact their performance as leaders.

## Millennial Working Style

Many millennials tend to live by this saying or some variation of this idea. They do not believe in the traditional organizational hierarchies as we know them or that one needs to be very experienced to be a leader. Millennials often believe that the best ideas can come from anywhere and can be acted upon whether or not they have been tested in the past, which is in fact the true spirit of teamwork in an organization. When they were new to the workforce, they would continuously challenge the status quo which would frustrate traditional management. As they step into leadership roles today, they aim to eradicate the very concept of having a status quo to begin with.

Very often, we see that millennials keep the end in mind, but are open to the way in which they go about achieving the goal. As highly mission-driven individuals, they believe that even if a strategy is charted it may not be the most sustainable way to run a business in real-time.

Additionally, in general, millennials and Gen Zers tend to gravitate to coworking spaces and unconventional office seating to do their best work at the time of day when their minds is actually primed to work. Having teams spread around the world, staying connected through tools such as Slack, Teams, WhatsApp and others is ideally and even preferred as millennial managers love the cultural diversity and global experience they receive while on the job.

The traditional practice of quarterly feedback reports and annual performance reviews could be helpful, but are often received in poor taste. Many millennials opt for real-time feedback and prefer day-to-day coaching over waiting months before checking in on individual progress.

In the end, everyone could benefit from making the transition in one respect or another to an open communication policy and a culture where feedback is shared and received authentically. The era in which many Gen Zers are growing up is forcing them to push boundaries in a way that their millennial parents did not. Baby boomers were content to structure the lives of their millennial children so they could be set up for the best success possible, but millennial parents are not so much on board with that way of life.

As more millennials take up leadership roles, the pendulum could swing back to an era of extremely high employee engagement and distinctly united and collaborative teams. Looking far beyond the idea of workforce segmentation and categorizing your workforce according to values, attitudes, and behaviours can set up companies for success and meet employees' expectations in ways that are meaningful and fruitful for the entire organization.

How do we get there? We start by focusing on three things:

- Speaking is done in real time.
- Listening is done in real time.
- Understanding is done through filters.

Open and effective communication in a safe environment at every level of the organization seems to be the major looming problem of our day that we must solve.

## Millennials and Miscommunication

What constitutes millennial communication?

Long phone calls? Detailed discussions over email? Not even close.

In general, millennials have a reputation for being the instant messaging, social messaging, text messaging generation. You can expect better communication through text messages and direct messages combined with more emoticons for expression than you would care to see in person. It is a communication characteristic that defines this demographic.

When a millennial enters a meeting, you can expect to see a laptop or tablet rather than a pen and paper, a video presentation over a PowerPoint, and perhaps, many jeans and a t-shirt over a full suit and tie. While he or she may be less experienced, they are no less equipped than their more senior peers – with the way in which information gets disseminated these days, they have a vast amount of resources at their disposal.

While this may seem like a major benefit to some, in today's workplace environment these could cause bigger headaches in our understanding of each other enough to work well.

Let's put this into perspective.

The Labor Force Composition report by the Pew Research Center found that the current U.S. workforce comprises of approximately 2% Traditionalists, 25% Baby Boomers, 33% Generation Xers, 35% Millennials and 5% Gen Z employees. Even though millennials constitute the majority of the workforce, the three preceding generations actually are in the majority when it comes to being in many decision-making leadership roles within their organizations. Millennials, however, can be considered the "middle managers" in the organizational chain. They often lead first line workers and receive guidance and directions from senior management above them. Sometimes, this can lead to miscommunication.

Taking a deep dive into this aspect, let's assume that millennial Mike sends a text message update about a current campaign to his baby boomer manager, Bobby. Chances are, Bobby hasn't even heard his phone ping and is logged in to his computer, staring at his inbox, waiting to receive the update from Mike.

This is one of the more common forms of miscommunication that arises in an office environment. This issue stems from a very deep root, far deeper than the misleading idea that millennials are simply always on their phones. It is true, millennials were raised in the age of digital connectivity. While this upbringing has made them highly skilled at all things technology, it has also stunted their interpersonal communication skills. Per a 2016 report by Bank of America, a whopping 39% of the 1000 millennials surveyed admit to having interacted more with their phones than the actual people in their lives.

Cross-generational communication is beginning to emerge as one of the primary factors that leads to an unhealthy workplace environment and a poor work culture. While modern society, pop culture and unconventional forms of child rearing have caused differences in the way employees in various generations think and communicate, studies prove that many of the goals, aspirations and workplace expectations are more similar between millennials and some of their peers than they are different.

Beyond that, diverse intelligences that allow for diverse opinions in an open and collaborative way make better decisions overall than homogenous intelligences. It follows that there is a lot that can be said about facilitating better communication across multiple generations.

For the baby boomer and Gen X manager, it is important to realize that when a millennial junior has an idea, it is not an attack on your ego, but could be a testament to good mentorship and cordial superior-subordinate relations. On the other hand, millennials must also understand that their older supervisors may not be as adept with newer platforms and systems that can result in more convenient ways of getting things done. Thus, it is critical to make the effort to meet halfway.

A truly communicative and collaborative workplace environment will only be built if these differences are acknowledged, understood, and embraced.

### The Real Problem

You would think after all you have read, we would have made it to the real problem already. The real problem is not that multiple generations of employees exist in the workplace. It is also not that there are many managers and leaders who aren't yielding better results with their employees. If you think hard about it, the real problem is not that employees of these many generations are having to unlearn and relearn elements of their work process.

The real problem that we face not only in our places of work but also in our world as a whole is simply understanding each other long enough to listen and grow. The year we were born into has largely determined how we communicate. But it is important to build a bridge with the current and next generation to not just coexist but to embrace the differences that make us unique.

I am reminded of a story with Captain Kirk and Spock. If you remember well, Captain Kirk proceeded to think of a plan to act the moment he identified the problem. Spock was at the ready to debate and run every occurrence through his formula for testing logical validity. And Scotty was busy putting the pedal to the metal. Neither was wrong – it was just the way in which they operated.

This is a humorous example, but it shows how three parties can be both different and right. It is finding how to connect in the correct way that will lead to a huge increase in relationship equity and performance.

In subsequent chapters, we will take a look at how we can mind the communication gap, build a bridge that connects previous, current, and future generations to each other, and develop our communication intelligence skills to create more effective and productive work environments – one in which our children and their children desire to be a part.

# CHAPTER 2

# It's Powerful – What Is Predictable Can Be Changed

If I were to ask what determines the success of a company, what typically comes to mind? Mission and vision. Revenue. Company size. Innovative products. Technology stack. Number of customers. Acquisitions.

These are all correct in their context, but the success of any company largely depends on how effectively team managers and team members communicate with each other. Communication, as we have already established, is one of the major causes for concern as millennials continue to climb the corporate ladder and take on mentorship and responsibility for the trajectory of incoming Gen Zers.

A survey conducted by 15Five reported that millennial employees are far more likely to feel ignored at work by the other generations around them. 30 percent of millennial respondents said their managers are often too busy to listen to them while another 30 percent said their managers didn't ask for employee feedback. 17 percent of those surveyed said even if they did offer feedback voluntarily, it would not be valued by their superiors.

If outcomes like this continue to be the state of workplace communication, it can easily lead to a very toxic workplace environment, an unwelcoming company culture, and high employee turnover rates.

The success of any company lies on the foundation of effective and honest communication. This type of communication leads to teamwork which can only be achieved when all employees are aligned to the same goals and understand a collaborative effort is always the answer. This high degree of alignment is only attained through great communication across multiple generations in the workplace.

Many years ago, when I was in-between jobs and minding my own business, having fun coaching my son's Pop Warner football team, I was approached by one of the other coaches who began to tell me about his new job and how he would love to have me on his team. Understand, my experience at that point had been in commercial real estate development and finance, not in sales.

So, very reluctantly, I accepted the position to sell a new medical technology to hospitals that non-invasively measured the volumetric changes in respiration. (I'm also not a scientist or medical professional so as you can imagine, this was not a good idea for either of us.)

PERSONAL CORE VALUE #1:

*A man needs to get up and be productive every day, personally and professionally.*

"A man needs to get up and be productive every day, personally and professionally."

However, I did learn that even a tiny change in respiration is the first indicator of a change in acuity. For good or bad, those indications could indicate un-monitored problems such as heart failure or show positive change to move the patient out of intensive care quicker and safer.

This is to say that the same holds true for communication. Communication is the first indicator of predictable behavior and if behaviors can be predicted, they can be changed to move stressful situations to very positive outcomes, helping people get out of the ICU (intensive communication unit).

## Effective Communication Changes the Game

The dynamics of the way businesses run are always changing. We are now stepping into a world where remote working, global teams, the gig economy and digital offices are not only trends but our new reality. The one thing that ties teams together and keeps companies functioning well is effective communication.

Imagine playing a game of ping-pong, but it is you versus the wall. Boring, right? Now imagine playing ping-pong with a friend or colleague and instantly, the game is not only better but is more fun. Your friend may even push you to play better too.

Now, try to imagine playing ping-pong with ten players and each one has a different size ball and paddle and someone who has no knowledge of ping-pong is keeping score!

Ensuring a work environment of effective communication has a similar effect on your team members. Work seems to be more fun and everyone is competing and pushing themselves to perform better. In more managerial terms, it builds morale within your teams.

The need for effective communication in the workplace is one of the reasons the Communication IQ™ assessment was created. If you haven't done so already, we would encourage you to scan the code at the back of this book to discover your top communication languages. The assessment can help you to process incoming and outgoing communication, better understand the way people prefer to think, feel, act and speak. Beyond that, it goes even deeper into your intensity level, acceptance level, internal level of control, leadership style, and susceptibility to stress. The better you understand your communication languages, the better you can communicate, and the sooner more effective and productive relationships can be cultivated.

When a team communicates effectively, the team members develop trust amongst each other because everyone feels like they are being heard, seen, and understood. Additionally, everyone is free to focus on what matters most within the organization. In a multi-generational environment, effective communication also helps to create a sense of belonging and inter-dependability which both act as pillars of harmony between employees.

Instilling a culture of open communication empowers employees to speak their minds and express ideas without fear. The exchange of ideas often leads to opportunities for innovation within your organization.

Whether the team is comprised of traditionalists and baby boomers in leadership, millennials in middle management, or a few Gen Z interns here and there, great communicators evolve when human understanding consists of listening, speaking, and understanding.

Communication is a lot more than simply getting your message across. It also includes knowing your team members individually and understanding how they receive information, spending time together and building trust, and allowing them the space to ask questions, disagree, and present new ways of thinking. It means making the conscious effort as a leader of a small or large organization or team to convert communication styles from lectures to healthy and engaging discussions.

## What is the Outcome of Effective Communication?

* Conflict resolution

The ability to speak, listen, and understand plays a major role in getting to root causes of problems and resolving conflicts amicably while preventing new ones from arising. Finding solutions that get everyone involved in the process allows each person to be responsible for sharing their perspectives and feelings, not necessarily agreeing with each other, and finding the right way to reduce unproductive outcomes.

* Offers clarity and a sense of direction

How often have you seen instructions given in a vague and ambiguous way. Everyone "hears" what was said but no one "understands" it. That is the way some of us communicate. Having effective communication skills allows us to not only deliver clear objectives and expectations but also to find constructive ways to identify what's wrong, what's missing, what's right, and what's confusing. Providing clarity and direction is important to millennials especially as they want to know what you expect so they can get it done. What is clear often gets done.

- Pay attention to the filters

Every person has a filter or lens through which they view every situation and conversation as well as other people involved. This lens extends subconscious messages that, when you are paying attention, will reveal hidden feelings and questions that are embedded in each individual perspective. Peter Drucker, a well-known management consultant said, "The most important thing in communication is to hear what isn't being said." We look at the world around us, the people in our environment, our supervisors and peers, and our workforce culture through these filters. Sometimes, the things we want to say don't actually get said. These filters can be one or many which is why it is important to not just hear, but to also understand.

- Room for Innovation

When employees are allowed to openly communicate their ideas and perspectives with the team without fear of retribution or ridicule, they are much more likely to make the effort to come to the table with their ideas. Innovation hinges upon multiple people encouraging communication and affirming each other toward progress.

*"To effectively communicate, we must realize that we are all different in the way we perceive the world and use this understanding as a guide to our communication with others."*
*—Anthony Robbins*

## Barriers to Effective Communication

It is very important to understand what the bottlenecks or barriers to effective communication are. In order to solve any problem, we must acknowledge there is a problem and understand its root cause.

31

There are several different kinds of barriers that lead to a communication gap in an organization. Let's start with the most obvious one – the generation barrier. People's experiences frame the way they perceive and communicate. Older generations of employees may have a tendency to disregard feedback from younger generations simply because they feel their experience has contributed to their decision. On the other hand, younger generations can sometimes, due to lack of experience, completely misread a situation or problem and act impulsively, costing a business hundreds, thousands, or even millions of dollars. This is why all teams need to understand better, listen better and communicate better.

I was reminded recently by one of my teenage grandkids that saying "all that and a bag of chips," "that's fly" or "the bomb.com," are no longer acceptable forms of validation. We have moved from "chips to lit." You should know these things!

Another very common barrier would literally be a physical barrier. If your boss is behind the doors of his corner office, you may get the perception that he is unwelcoming or not available to talk. A similar issue arises when colleagues have cubicles. The walls are built to prevent unwanted distraction, but sometimes end up preventing meaningful discussions. This is why most modern offices have an open floor concept. The office setup contributes to the work culture and can be part of the difference that determines whether or organization is innovative and productive.

Other barriers that impact effective communication in the workplace are psychological barriers such as low employee morale due to stressful work conditions, unrealistic targets, routine work, workplace bullying, and similar issues stemming from a toxic work culture and environment.

Awareness of all these barriers is crucial, as it will help identify why a particular problem is occurring and how management can deal with it better.

## Planning for Effective Communication

In subsequent chapters, we will dive deep in how you can ensure your work environment enables effective communication among employees vertically and horizontally.

There are few basic techniques to make sure the environment is conducive to open communication. To begin with, managers, bosses, team leaders and supervisors must lead in a manner in which their understudies never refrain or think twice before approaching them.

Another great way to do so is to hold face-to-face meetings or open forums as opposed to text messages or email. As a manager, you must be available to meet the needs of your team members, not just to make sure they are meeting their targets and hitting their numbers, but to ensure they are receiving communication in the way they prefer and thriving in an environment that is conducive to their progress and success.

PERSONAL CORE VALUE #2:
*"Real leaders don't need a title; they need trust."*

Real leaders don't need a title; they need trust.

One of my first jobs in real-estate management was running a mega mall in Texas. As a 25-year-old, I was perceived as a "young whipper snapper." By who? Older retail executives who had dedicated their lives to building successful big box stores. I certainly couldn't tell them anything, and therefore, they elected not to participate in lease requirements including merchants associations.

Rather than getting lawyers involved and creating conflict and financial consequences, I decided to take a different route. The ring leader of this intelligence was a 70-year-old man who was not ever going to agree or support anything I wanted to accomplish. So, I asked to have a breakfast meeting with him, and he obliged. It occurred to me that this man had decades of retail experience and really wanted to be a mentor to a humble 25-year-old whipper snapper.

It was the humble part that I stumbled over. Once I swallowed my pride and turned down the arrogance, he and I began to build a relationship which led to him listening a little more, and over a very short period of time, his influence changed the game with all the others. From that time on, he led the charge for me, even agreeing to pay for flying Santa Claus in on a helicopter!

One critical thing to keep in mind is that meetings must be meaningful. Millennials especially have an aversion to meaningless and lengthy meetings. It is not that they hate meetings, but they will be more engaged if they are productive, meaningful and brief.

Additionally, dispel the 9-5 work day notion and the idea that in order to get ahead one has to be available 24/7. One of the biggest drivers for millennials is to be able to view and participate in the bigger picture of work outside of "working hours." The more involved they feel and connected to the holistic side of work-life balance, the better they will perform.

Now that we have covered the basic understanding of how important effective communication is and that great communicators evolve when they learn to listen, speak, and understanding, let's take a look at some keys to effective listening and speaking.

# CHAPTER 3

# Listening and Speaking

Stephen R. Covey once said, *"Most people do not listen with the intent to understand; They listen with the intent to reply."*

Isn't this true of most of us.

"Two ears and one mouth." I guess that's better than one ear and two mouths although I have run into some folks that seem like their talking from two different...well never mind.

PERSONAL CORE VALUE #3:

*Listen first, assimilate second, include third, don't make crap up fourth.*

Listen first, assimilate second, include third, don't make crap up fourth.

The common communication structure within our modern world revolves around impulsive replies and wanting to be right in our answers. Millennials have been well touted as a generation focused on debates and rebuttals rather than mutual conversations. But before we dig deeper into this, let's seek to understand the art of listening and speaking.

## Understanding How to Listen

By definition, listening is the active process by which we make sense of, assess, and respond to what we hear. However, when we talk about the art of listening, what we refer to is active listening.

Active listening is a communication technique that requires the listener to not only provide feedback to the speaker based on what he or she has heard, but also to fully concentrate on what is being said and to remember it after it has been said. This means you put your undivided focus on what the speaker is saying – physically and mentally.

## The Art of Speaking Right

The act of speaking means translating your thoughts into words and saying them out loud. Despite being a simple act, most people really do have a hard time speaking their minds. Beyond that, many people have a hard time accepting what is spoken from someone else as well.

Why is that?

This is because, more often than not, we speak without having our minds fully engaged in the process.

The art of speaking right is much more than speaking when spoken to and replying when asked a question. Speaking right means you understand time, place, context, and sensitivity. It means sticking to your point even if it is not popular and being clear in what you want from the people around you. Clarity of thought is critical if we are to speak right.

**Listening and Speaking Across Generations**

Irrespective of which generation of employees you are categorized into, the major issues around why most communication efforts fail remain the same –

1. Inactive listening

2. Mindless speaking

**Communication Evolution**

If we talk about workplace communication from an evolutionary perspective, traditionalists were really the last generation that relied solely on face to face conversations, phone calls, sticky notes and letters.

Baby boomers grew up when the telephone transitioned from a bulky and expensive device to smaller units that the average person could afford. However, these were still fairly expensive and not everyone had one. Hence, we find more often than not that most baby boomers still prefer face to face conversations and would probably drop in an email or two along the way.

A survey presented at the Americas Conference on Information Systems found that 93 percent of baby boomer respondents used e-mail on a daily basis. Having said that, Gen X was really the first generation to adopt email as a primary means of communication. Email is quicker and more efficient. There is always a trail of what was being said from the receiver and the sender, but there was always a portion of meaning and intent that could get lost in translation.

A study from NTT Data confirmed that email is Gen X's preferred form of communication, whether at work or at home.

Another major difference between Gen X employees and baby boomer employees is that in general, Gen Xers prefer short, to the point messaging within email. For many Gen Xers, if it can't be read quickly in an email, it might not need to be sent. In the military, there is something called Army Standard when it comes to writing. The five elements of effective writing for military leaders are: to be concise, to be clear, to have correct mechanics, to use the active voice, and to ensure the bottom line is up front. This is interesting to remember when writing emails next time to a Gen Xer.

## Millennials and Gen Z

It is the responsibility of company leaders to make sure they adapt to their Gen Z employees while respecting their current baby boomer employees, who may be more seasoned in their careers and less familiar with the tech-savvy ways of their new co-workers.

According to a report by Ryan Jenkins, 72 percent of Gen Z respondents want to communicate face-to-face at work. This is absolutely different from millennials who are always looking for ways to have text message interactions and will not understand why their older counterparts are quite late to the game.

Millennials will now find themselves needing to straddle the fence carefully and work along a high-tech and high-touch model in the workplace to ensure the baby boomers ahead of them are stable and secure, and that the Gen Z employees under them are motivated and happy, as more than 90% of Gen Z respondents stressed the importance of having a human element at work.

Millennials will need to keep in mind that Gen Z grew up with tools such as YouTube and various learning resources that are only a few clicks away. Therefore, Gen Z employees expect to have a truly seamless and effortless experience with their work.

Customization is critical and whether it is on-demand and on the cloud – Gen Zers expect everything to be compactly accessible on their mobile devices.

This is where the speaking and the listening across the generations in the workplace can get foggy. The manager of today's workforce must seek to not only be heard and understood himself but must also seek to hear and understand those who are speaking to him on his team – directly or indirectly. I think it is safe to say that listening is a lost art and if brought back into our world, could make a big difference in our current and future success.

Millennials and Gen Z are used to having access to whatever they want, whenever they want. They pull information up on mobile devices and listen to podcasts on their way to work. They value things like videos that can provide quick bursts of information on the go.

Since they are such a digital generation, Gen Z generally lacks the interpersonal skills that come naturally to older members of the workforce. Thus, Gen Z will look to millennials to help them engage in critical thinking and strategic speaking. It is important for baby boomer and millennial bosses to familiarize themselves with other perspectives, topics, and ideas to effective work around them.

One of the biggest differences between millennials and Gen Z is that there are no clear boundaries between work and life for Gen Z. As more of this generation enters the workforce, they'll need to carefully designate where work stops and where life picks up. This invisible line will vary from person to person, but it's critical to find this line of demarcation to ensure they don't get burnt out. Millennials, being the generation that stresses upon a healthy work-life balance, will be responsible for ensuring this critical shift as well.

As millennials slowly take up leadership positions in organizations and Gen Zers join those teams, it is becoming more important to create a culture of seamless and effective communication. Ineffective communication affects employees and their work deeply, as it creates a lack of trust and poor collaboration.

So how can we ensure that we become better communicators? Let's find out.

**Improving Communication**

I thought my new car phone in the 80's was going to do several things. First, I thought it would prove my communication was so important that I could not be unconnected. Second, I thought it would prove I was so important that you should do business with me. Third, I thought it would prove that I was cool. What I quickly discovered was that none of those were true.

Great communication isn't about you. Its' about others and having spoken in front of thousands over my professional career, the most positive feedback I ever got wasn't based on delivery or technology but what was caught in personal application. People get more from what is caught than what is taught.

How can both baby boomers and millennials improve communication skills at work, and make sure they are truly listening and speaking well?

Here are a few basic measures that organizations can take to ensure more holistic communication:

1. Make personal connections a priority

Organizations must ensure that in this fast and progressive digital age, employees do not miss out on the human element. After all, relationships cannot be built in megabytes and gigabytes. Therefore, face-to-face meetings must be held at times that work for your organization. This could be an annual gathering or more frequently, ever six months or every quarter. This will make sure teams are internally and collectively working towards the same objectives and that harmony exists. This will also help reduce errors due to a failure to listen or speak well – miscommunication.

## 2. Engage in active listening

Active listening will help employees improve their interpersonal relationships and have the holistic needs of the team as well as individual needs met. Companies must ensure that they train their employees to engage in mindful communication practices. A very common trend is for companies to have meditation rooms on site, so when employees feel too overwhelmed by the workload, they can simply realign their focus. Additionally, some newer companies are allocating monthly funds for remote teams to have access to yoga sessions and other spaces for quiet time and meditation. Most importantly, some employees need to be encouraged to be more inquisitive. The work environment needs to be such that they feel free to ask questions for clarification, or even share ideas for further discussion without receiving the side-eye from their bosses or peers.

## 3. Practice self-awareness

It is always so much more easier to highlight another person's bad qualities instead of checking one's own. For this purpose, many companies hire performance coaches and psychiatrists as consultants or in-resident members of the team to help team members open up their minds and embark upon a journey of self-awareness. How do you communicate? How do the majority of your team communicate? How well do you listen? Do people typically understand what you mean when you speak to them? This and other similar questions can guide the self-awareness journey. On the converse, this can help companies understand if they're doing anything wrong or if they can do some things better.

Several years ago, one of our senior consultants was invited to take part in a "cattle call" for a company that was experiencing very large turnover rates. So, the CEO decided that each potential consultant would get 15 minutes to describe how they would fix his problem. Our consultant got the allotted 15 minutes and because of the training and understanding of how to listen and respond, it became very evident that this was part of, if not most of the problem. Our 15 minutes turned into a three-year relationship that is still active today. And the company is experiencing a transformation in its communication culture which by the way has reduced turnover and saved massive talent costs.

4. Measure accountability through continuous feedback

Quarterly review meetings could soon be a thing of the past as younger employees are more demanding and expect more from themselves at work. Millennials often ask their older peers for feedback on critical projects that are important to the company. If not given a clear path for this, they will insist on having face to face time with their leaders and understanding how they can get better at their jobs in real time. This will then become more of a weekly or bi-monthly experience.

Aside from this, employees also need to actively take steps to communicate better. If good communication – listening and speaking – do not become part of the corporate culture, it will lead to larger issues including retention and engagement.

Here are a few guidelines we can follow on an individual level:

1. Be present

Great communication, good workplace relationships, work satisfaction, and feeling a sense of purpose – all can be achieved by practicing mindfulness and being present in the moment. Mindfulness, very simply put, means living in the NOW and we can be present with each other when we choose to speak and listen. Being truly present in the moment will make you appreciate the value of the human experience.

2. Pay attention

We often think that communication is only what we hear. However, we need to know that gestures, expressions and movements are all incredibly essential parts of a wholesome, meaningful and productive conversation. Pay attention to the nonverbal cues – head nods, facial expressions, raised eyebrows, vocal tone, body posture, hand gestures, and physical distance. These small signs sometimes give you more information than words ever could.

3. Avoid hesitation when the understanding, objective or perspective isn't clear

Perspective and understanding is a tricky thing to handle. You may think someone meant something, when in reality they probably meant something else or that they have said something when they meant to say something totally different. To avoid misunderstanding what has been said or intended, be sure to clarify the message you have received before proceeding. Learn to ask questions. Get comfortable with obtaining clarification and ensuring all parties are on the same page. Few things are worse than when a team has left a meeting with ten different interpretations about what has been said.

This is why active listening is important and active clarification as well. Don't hesitate to ask for your clarity. Steve Maraboli said "It's a lack of clarity that creates chaos and frustration. Those emotions are poison to any living goal." Similarly, as leaders, do not hesitate to convey the same point more than once in different forums and channels so every team member on your team understands.

## Benefits of Listening and Speaking Appropriately

Once the organization and the employees work through these points, you will definitely see a change in your work environment and in team engagement and productivity. There are many ways in which it will change your office atmosphere and how employees feel about being at work. Some of them include:

### 1. Trust

Once employees and managers are able to communicate openly and freely, it creates an atmosphere of trust within the organization. This is crucial to building collaborative efforts and achieving the organization's goals. This also improves the employer brand and attracts the best talent to the company. Employees will feel mentored by their managers and empowered by their peers. The result: retention rates will rise. Gen Z employees need to know they are adding value since huge salary packages aren't everything for them. Millennials will be able to shape many young minds, which will also drive them to perform better and feel meaningful in their jobs.

### 2. Enhanced Productivity

When communication improves, information is passed on better and faster. Once employees have all the information they need to get the job done, they will be able to do so faster. This massively increases productivity levels in your organization and can lead to a lingering healthy competition among employees. What better way to check off all of the company's objectives?

3. Reduces and resolves conflicts

Having an open communication system in the workplace means that miscommunication can be reduced, and misunderstandings are less frequent and resolved faster. This will be very beneficial, as workplace conflicts often defer focus and involvement. This will also give rise to higher employee engagement and satisfaction levels. When concerns are heard and resolved faster, teams tend to work better.

4. An environment of mutual respect

When employees and managers communicate better, they are able to forge stronger bonds and relationships within the workplace. Everyone feels respected and driven to do their best work and bring their best selves to work. Triggering employees' internal push factors is sometimes the goal for managers. But when this drive is motivated fully internally, everyone seeks to understand and be clear when speaking.

## Communicating Across Generations

As we have established by now, every generation has its own preferred way of communicating. There is nothing wrong with either communication style but in a cross-generational workplace like the one we live in today, merging all of these and finding a way to really bring everyone together is key. Here are a few ways this can be done:

1. Know Your Audience

Know the proportion of the number of employees from each generation on your team and design your communication strategies, tools and technologies accordingly. In some cases, if the teams are too diverse, you may need to tailor conversations to match peers, managers, or subordinates.

Meeting with a baby boomer manager may call for a more formal tone, while a conversation with a Gen Z or millennial could be more relaxed, held in the break room or over email or text.

### 2. Customize Your Message

We discussed earlier how each generation prefers and naturally communicates. Sometimes, there may be outliers – misfits, non-conformists – the ones who break the mold. It is necessary to understand the best communication style for such team members and adjust your communication with them accordingly.

### 3. Adapt to Change

As millennials take on leadership roles and Gen Z joins their teams, Baby Boomers and Gen X need to ensure they are adapting to the change and keeping up with the present communication styles. After all, change is the only constant. It does not mean you fail to be who you are. But the way to bridge the gap and communicate effectively is if we actively seek to learn the newer ways of preferred communication and work towards meeting our younger employees halfway. It is not far-fetched to do so either. Our own children are millennials and Gen Z who also communicate in this way. It may frustrate us at home but could stifle our business in the work environment.

Executives, managers, supervisors, team leaders and employees must all actively seek and listen to feedback and perspectives on different aspects of the organization and how work is done. This helps to minimizes chaos, confusion, and hurt feelings and offers a sense of community, validation, and acceptance to the younger leaders. Active listening and mindful speaking can, therefore, be great morale boosters in the workplace. However, these aren't the only ingredients you need to blend.

In the next chapter, we talk about two more essential components that will help you achieve great levels of open communication and collaboration in the workplace: hearing and understanding.

# CHAPTER 4

# Hearing and Understanding

PERSONAL CORE VALUE #4:

*Don't let schedules become substance abuse.*

In this day and age, employees spend more time with their colleagues and teammates than they do with their spouses and children. In reality, our work lives have become more time consuming and demanding than we would like to admit or accept sometimes.

48

If this is the case, then it is safe to assume that we are also communicating more with our colleagues than with our family members and friends. Don't think so? Check your recent call logs or text messages and it is possible that this is true.

It is becoming more important than ever to develop more meaningful relationships at our places of work, since according to data shared by Jessica Pryce-Jones in *Happiness at Work,* "the average person will spend approximately 90,000 hours at work across their lifespan." Because of this, many HR managers and company executives stress the importance of having an environment of open and authentic communication at work.

How is this consistently possible? Through learning to hear and understand each other better.

In the last chapter, we learned about two pillars needed to effectively communicate at work: Listening and Speaking. In this chapter, we will cover the last two pillars that are critical for a solid foundation in communication: Hearing and Understanding.

### Hearing – How to Do It Right?

We hear a lot of people talk about a lot of things over the course of our lifetime. But, how often do we really hear what they are saying? Not just the words coming out of their mouth, but also the tone, intensity, emotion, intention, and meaning of what they are saying?

The process of really hearing what another person is saying involves 3 considerations which we will briefly discuss:

1. Kinetic Intelligence

2. Emotive Intelligence

3. Cognitive Intelligence

Our cognitive processes include all efforts made in order to listen to what the speaker is saying, isn't saying, and processing the words to understand the true meaning and intent of what has been said. Our affective processes are where our human interests, biases, and preferences have an impact on how we process information. This is where we start further thinking about and processing the information we've received, adding our perceptions, perspectives, and beliefs that help to form our opinions.

Our behavioral processes refer to the decisions we take when acting or reacting after we have received some information – either positive or negative. We tend to take a physical action (tantrums), an emotional reaction (angry outburst), or cognitive action (thinking negatively). Whatever action or reaction we choose to have is determined in this stage.

Hearing is a three step process which entails a number of reactions to what is being heard. In simple terms, you must first listen to the words being spoken, break down what has been heard, map what you understand and think has been intended to what you already know, and then decide what to do with that information.

### Differences in the Perspectives of Each Generation

Irrespective of the differences, one thing that is a common thread across all the generations is that nobody is willing to work just a "regular job." With that being said, there are certain differences that must be acknowledged to ensure a collaborative and cohesive working experience.

As the younger generations have been raised in the age of advancing technology, they are naturally better at handling the technology that is often needed to run businesses well. This means older generations must be open to either learning new technologies themselves (which in some cases could be a massive learning curve) or give autonomy and space with affirmation to their younger peers to guide certain initiatives.

One major difference between older and younger generations is that younger employees often do not wish to follow in the footsteps of their older colleagues. Rather than choosing to follow routine career paths, they tend to continuously challenge the status quo and often find nothing wrong with skipping out on a job they no longer love. Traditionalists and baby boomers, for instance, entered the workforce with the idea that they would have one career and possibly just one employer throughout their lifetime and thus loyalty and compromise became orders of the day. Gen X was prepared to work for a number of employers, but most likely in the same fields throughout their careers. However, millennials are open to changing jobs and careers especially if it provides them with the flexibility and autonomy they desire. Being more exploratory in nature, it's the learning and mentorship that drives them.

As an older generation of managers and company leaders, it is important that we hear our younger counterparts out not only in interviews but also in meetings and break room conversations. The way we bridge the communication gap between generations is by not only speaking and listening well but also by hearing and understanding well. When we hear and understand in a way that is effective and collaborative, we open the door for major change in the way we communicate and become more productive in helping each other become better people.

When it comes to our Gen Z generation, they are the least measured in their approach. They tend to make sure they have both a learning curve to achieve and a future prospect where they are working. Unafraid to take risk and not entirely committed to loyalty as we know, they tend to manage their side hustles as their day jobs and often explore various fields in their career. They believe learning can be derived from any resource, but mentorship and experience help to accelerate their careers.

Both Millennials and Gen Z consider mentorship as an essential part of their overall development. As business demographics continue to change, the need to adopt newer learning strategies is more important than ever. Therefore, communication is key to facilitate the two-way mentorship between the older and younger generations. Both sides have to learn to hear each other and understand.

Therefore, what really matters at work is not differences in perspectives, but the understanding that these differences exist and are instrumental to who we are and how we think. At the crux of the entire dilemma lies the fact that younger employees care about performance quality and often judge their managers by the content of their work. What they tend to demand in return is to not be judged for their hours but for their results.

When communicating about work with their younger peers, managers must take a transparent, honest and personalized approach. They must always seek to understand the benefits employees want to receive.

Millennials and Gen Z employees value career development, but also feel there must be work-life balance in the mix. Squeezed between Gen X and Gen Z, millennials are generally more educated, self-reliant and hardworking. They are comfortable using technology and comfortable interacting with humans without the interference of a screen. As a result, they can be used to bridge the gap between tech-savvy individuals and the tech-deprived older employees.

Gen X employees often facilitate the creation of an environment with a more individualistic emphasis on where and how they can work, be inspired and be pushed to do and become better. They initiated an era of greater autonomy for employees. However, on the flip side, this also means more accountability and a bit more stress than before. Members of this generation strive to achieve a healthy work-life balance.

Focusing on these top fundamental drivers and boosters can help companies attract and retain employees across all generations. The multi-generational workforce offers significant advantages to managers and team leaders with regards to designing the scope of experience and innovative critical thinking aptitudes.

It is imperative for managers to develop and design an office space that suits the engagement of all the employees. We must incorporate a great blend of digital and traditional office practices. We must also leverage experiences of the older employees to train younger employees so they too can gain understanding of the history behind the ways in which we work. We are also responsible for making sure younger employees are patient and compassionate while helping older employees. This can be accomplished by developing mentoring and coaching programs to pass down information, perspectives, and best practices. By focusing on communication and understanding the priorities of each generation, organizations will definitely be able to achieve their goals in the most sustainable manner.

## Understanding Across Generations

In the process of effective communication, we discussed how we listen and speak to each other. When we are listening, we use the process of hearing to appropriately decipher the information that has been received. We have also discussed how differently each generation in the workplace communicates, what drives them and how communication preferences evolve over the decades. Additionally, we have discussed how important it is to truly understand what is being said, and how much of an impact it can have in the workplace.

Let's now take a look at how we can seek to facilitate this in a workplace environment.

One major facilitator of communication in a cross-generational workforce is technology. As each of the generations has been through their own stage of technology evolution, it is important to understand that every employee will not have the same pace of hearing and understanding. Therefore, we will start by categorizing the workforce not by generation but by their style and preference of communication.

From my years of leading workshops and coaching sessions to help managers, teams, and organizations to better communicate, we've found that communication preferences and styles can be categorized into seven different types. None of these are right or wrong, and each person speaks all seven in different ranges and intensities, but it is helpful to understand each type to better understand how we communicate and how others like to be communicated to around us.

### Movers™

Movers are those employees who instinctively become leaders. They automatically take charge in situations and often tend to believe in the mantra, "Lead, follow, or get out of the way."

### Doers™

Doers are the employees who do not really care about who the leader is. To a Doer, doing their work and checking items off of their to-do lists is of topmost importance. Doers have an eye for detail in most cases and are true believers in collaborative effort.

### Influencers™

Influencers are the lifeline of almost every office. They celebrate every victory, every good day at work and make sure employee morale is high. They also tend to motivate their colleagues with a positive attitude and keep employee conflict at a minimum.

### Responders™

Responders are the employees who find their true calling and passionately follow it. Often involved with volunteering and charitable efforts, responders make sure there is more meaning to their lives than just the typical 9-5.

### Shapers™

You would usually find that your organization's top-level executives fit the category of the Shaper. They are always trying to stay ahead of the curve and tend to be in position to think several steps ahead of the competition. Shapers have a natural calling for strategy and organizational vision.

### Producers™

Producers are the ones who tend to strive for excellence and perfection in their efforts. In many cases, they are the employees who are the most efficient and effective especially in areas such as managing funds and allocating resources where needed the most.

### Contemplators™

Contemplators are as the name suggests the ones who tend to think through things more than anyone else on the team. They tend to consider all sides and believe that possessing knowledge is the most important thing. Knowledge is what drives them, and in many cases, they are calm, peaceful and collected no matter how chaotic the situation may be.

Once you know how your employees process and engage communication and the order of languages they speak, you can better understand what drives them, how they think and feel, what matters most to them, and how to communicate in an effective manner with them.

### The Massive Dilemma, Or Is It?

Given how much time employees spend together, the development of good relationships in the workplace is a byproduct of learning to hear and understand each other.

I call this Relationship Equity.

Coworkers become friends and look forward to spending time with one another while they work which can be reminiscent of school days for younger employees – all of this can be a reality for your organization as well.

The key is to ensure that the work environment facilitates open communication between employees of all generations and across all levels of the organizational hierarchy. This means that employees of the older generation must be open to guiding those of the younger generation through their experiences, as well as being open to ideas, feedback, perspectives, and suggestions from them. Similarly, while the younger employees reap the benefits of mentorship, they must make sure they are also doing their part and helping the older generation understand the modern perspectives and ways of being more efficient and effective with technology.

It is safe to say that the reality isn't as binary and bleak as it has been projected to be all these years. Baby boomers and Gen Xers are extensively adopting newer forms of technology and open to learning as technology becomes more accessible and part of their daily lives. As a result, bridging the communication gap is not actually as difficult as it may look.

# CHAPTER 5

# We Aren't That Far Apart

PERSONAL CORE VALUE #5:
*Leaders don't focus on a gap; they focus on a bridge.*

One of our prospective clients decided in our negotiations that we were too far apart to make things work. I asked a simple question: "Are you willing to do the work to create an opportunity to move forward?"

The answer was yes so rather than focusing on how far the gap was, I began to focus on changing objections to opportunities.

Each one became another pillar in the bridge. When things got dicey or rough, I reminded them that we had committed to work toward an opportunity.

The results took several days, but in the end, we built the bridge. It wasn't as tall as I wanted, but it wasn't as far as they thought.

In the last few chapters, we have talked about the dynamics and demographics of our current workforce that has changed drastically with baby boomers at the helms of companies and boards, millennials quickly approaching those positions, and Gen Zers coming through the doors at steady rates.

We also identified various categories in which we can learn to place ourselves and those with whom we work– movers, doers, influencers, responders, shapers, producers and contemplators. Each of these categories represent a particular communication style and language that we all tend to speak in descending order of language, qualities, intensities, and range. The more we seek to understand each of those languages, the better we can communicate with those around us and the better we can respond to those who communicate with us.

As a manager or leader within your company who has or will work with cross-generational team members, it is very important for you to be able to understand the communication language that best suits your employees at an individual level and as a team at a collective level. Having this knowledge is tremendously helpful to ensuring your employees understand how and where they fit and thrive best, but also how their peers and managers fit and thrive best as well as how to see the big picture within the organization.

In this chapter, we will dive into how close we really are to the generations behind and ahead of us. It seems we are far apart in the ways in which we choose to communicate, and to be honest, the media and society can make us think that we are far apart as well. In reality, however, we are not that far from each other. We can make the effort to hear, listen and understand and when we do, it makes the people around us better and the environments in which we live, work, and play amazing places to be.

## Communicate Using the Appropriate Language with the Appropriate People

As we have established, each individual team member has a particular communication language that is largely dependent on the character and personality traits each of us possess. When I talk about a language, I do not refer to the language in which we speak, such as English, Spanish, French, and Hindi. The lingo we are born into continues to evolve just as often as our generations change. Terms that were common a decade ago are considered ancient today and vice-versa.

Instead, when I say language, I am referring to the tone and content of the language we use. It is part character, part personality, part interactivity (reactions, actions, and responses), and part cognitive. We've discussed each of the 7 communication styles outlined in the Communication IQ™ assessment briefly in a previous chapter. But it is a good idea for you to take a few minutes and take the assessment which you will find a link to at the back of the book. It will take you deeper into your languages and styles of communication and it will give you practicable tips to apply your newfound knowledge to your everyday work environment.

For now, let's look further into what appeals to each of these communication styles and how you as a manager or leader within your company can leverage this concept to create more open communication in your workplace, increase engagement, reduce conflict and ultimately reduce turnover to improve your ROI.

Before we look at each communication style or language, remember every person speaks them all and with minimal training can bring bottom tier languages up significantly

### Mover™

People who speak Mover as a primary language are innovative, productive and often think outside of the box. In whatever role they play, they tend to lead the charge and find the quickest way toward action and progress. The way to ensure that you are receiving their undivided attention is by showing clarity of thought and crystal clear points of action.

People who speak the Mover communication language are often excited about discussing ideas and strategies. They also tend to rely on what is instinctive and constantly look for new challenges to tackle. Once you know what drives a Mover, you can shift your focus to staying out of the details when a Mover is the receiver of information and spotlight the big picture.

Movers prefer straightforward, direct communication. Talk without action is confusing to someone who speaks Mover language and can result in nothing getting done. Movers often have to develop patience and be responsible at times for the details of a project so that it ultimately gets completed.

### Doer™

People who speak the Doer communication language first are as the name suggests, about getting things done and getting them done right. Doers are practical, diligent and detail-oriented. They focus more on the work that is being done and whether the needs around them are being met.

Your utility matters more to a Doer than your rank in the company's hierarchy. This could translate into words meaning nothing until action supports it. When talking to a Doer, it is important to ensure that you are appreciating their efforts and stating clear action points that need to get done. Doers tend to be extremely trustworthy and loyal, are not prone to small talk, work well behind the scenes, maintain a high level of energy and often finish what they start.

To communicate well with a Doer, be sure to tell them what the expected course of action is. Doers manage their lives and will guard your plans and objectives to the finish.

### Influencer™

People who speak the Influencer communication language are often naturally gifted in their craft or have years of experience. They are highly intuitive, inclusive of new ideas and philosophies, and extremely enthusiastic about their role at work and in life.

To a person who speaks Influencer, team work is more important and they need all parties to be connected to the cause and mission as well as affirmative in their approach. They tend to see the glass as half full and overflowing and will spread any message in an encouraging and acceptable way that gets the team onboard and engaged.

This type of employee is a natural born motivator and encourager. They often love to talk but are not the most diplomatic at times with their words. To communicate best with a person who speaks Influencer, being creative and encouraging is the best way to get your message across.

### Responder™

People who speak the Responder communication language are often caring and compassionate. They tend to be creative and goal-oriented. They also often desire to touch the lives of people who are in need and/or who are hurting.

You need to convince the people around you who speak Responder at times that you understand their ideas and points of view. Their key drivers are to protect, and to advocate for causes they believe in, sometimes making them textbook people pleasers. Responders must feel deeply passionate about their jobs and often lead with their emotions.

Letting them know you are appreciative of their work and their attitude towards their work and the people around them will compel them to work harder. To communicate with those on your team who speak Responder, you must ensure that they feel like you care for them and have unconditional acceptance of them.

### Shaper™

People who speak the Shaper communication language tend to be the most senior executives of a company. As a manager or leader within an organization, it is crucial to know how to handle conflicts and communication with colleagues, subordinates and superiors.

With someone who speaks Shaper, it helps to understand that they speak, think, and talk strategy and planning. To communicate with them well, be prepared to share the key points, rebuttals and ideas with them. Shapers tend to have plans for years into the future and often seek to progressively move in an upward trajectory.

When talking to a Shaper, seek to present your line of thinking with clarity and be sure that it supports and helps to drive the Shaper's bigger picture. Shapers tend to be CEOs and company leaders and are driven by mentoring and developing their team members and guiding them towards the future.

Shapers are patient, which allows them to think several steps ahead of everybody else. Shapers think everyone should have a plan for their lives, so it is best if you also have one when communicating with them.

### Producer™

People who speak the Producer communication language are often financially adept and resourceful. They often watch the bottom line and have a very generous nature. They tend to lead quiet lives and be more reserved in their thought and communication.

When talking to someone who speaks Producer, it is important to be efficient and effective. Slip in words of appreciation of their efforts as it helps them to feel motivated in their work. While they have great financial acumen, their resourcefulness is what makes them who they are. As a manager, it is critical to make use of these characteristics.

To communicate well with a Producer, make sure you show forth trust, responsibility and empowerment. A Producer has to feel that the people around them are people to whom delegation can be given. They are very generous, but they sense irresponsibility and stinginess a mile away.

## Contemplator™

People who speak the Contemplator communication language are often looking to gain more and new knowledge. They are the thinkers within a company who tend to think intensively about the matters around them. Often, Contemplators gain satisfaction from being able to obtain new knowledge even more so than impressing people with their knowledge.

These life-long learners and lovers of books often need to "feel" something a hundred percent before they can participate productively. They are typically brilliant people, have high IQs, and prefer relatively low or zero environments of conflict and tension. Once they think through fully what they want to do and have all the information they need to do it, Contemplators can also be high achievers.

To communicate with Contemplators on your team, let them figure out the "WHY" behind a project or initiative before asking for their thoughts. If you do, they will show you results and outcomes that you may have never anticipated. Keeping a balance between work and life is also important so avoid stressful, last minute needs and requests from a Contemplator. They march to a drumbeat of their own.

After reading through each of these different types of communication languages and styles on your team, it is evident an understanding of these are needed to communicate effectively.

Let's focus on how we can learn 4 keys that drive each communication language:

- **Key #1: Filter –** Figure out what it is that the person really seeks in a conversation.

- **Key #2: Need –** Identify what drives the person.

- **Key #3: Spark** – Once you find what drives them, that is the button you need to press to keep them motivated.

- **Key #4: Validate Strength** – Once you have pressed the right button, remind them of their core strength and assure them they can do it.

### How Far Are You?

Long story short, we really are not that far apart from each other!

Don't believe me?

Well, let me get you to think about that for a minute. I want you to recollect the information from the previous chapters. Think about the different personalities, drivers, needs, filters, attributes, and communication languages and styles involved.

You will notice that you already have all the ingredients you need to be effective, efficient, productive, and happy –

✓ Employees – check

✓ Bosses – check

✓ Profiles – check

✓ Organizational goals and objectives – check

✓ Mission, vision and purpose – check

✓ Motivators – check

So what's missing?

What has been missing historically is the link – finding out who, why and how people connect and communicate best. Once you have completed the assessment (which can be found at the end of this book) to understand your Communication IQ™ profile, the communication language you speak and those around you speak, you will discover some ways in which to not only communicate better, but understand the healthy and unhealthy communication habits that can be appreciated and developed.

From the point of view of your team members and employees, if their manager is able to communicate well with them, it will generate a sense of trust, belonging, and understanding – all of which are pillars upon which open communication is built. This means that employees will allow their supervisors to guide them, mentor them, teach them, help them win, and encourage them in moments of challenge.

We can all agree by now that effective communication doesn't just happen. It happens when it is intentional. We can also agree that good communicators are not just born, although some of them are. Good communication is a skill that can be crafted and learned over time. You can get better at communicating with your managers, your peers, your coworkers, those you teach, mentor, and lead.

The right way to do this is to get back to the basic fundamentals of communication. Assess your teams, categorize them accurately, understand how they think, what they want, how they work, why they do things the way they do – and to get the 4 keys right. Making an intentional and conscious effort initially will pay off continuously. Today, it is called relationship equity.

**The Payoff**

Want to know if the tassel is worth the hassle?

Well, the first and most obvious outcomes of your efforts would be a steady flow of communication that spans beyond words, as members of the emoji and GIF era are able to freely and openly communicate with the ones who grew up completely wireless.

A Smarp.com report shows that 4 in every 5 employees claim internal communication in an organization impacts their job performance. Tribal Impact said that 74% of employees feel they are out of the loop or missing out on company news.

IBM also concluded that a whopping 72% of employees do not fully understand the strategy of the companies for which they work.

A McKinsey & Company report said employee productivity increases by a massive 20% to 25% in organizations where employees are well connected.

Think Talent found that companies that have effective communication programs in place were 3.5 times more likely to outperform their rivals.

As humans have evolved, our communication styles have also evolved. As businesses continue to evolve in this technology driven age, employees and communication styles need to be understood. It would be wonderful to live in a world where everyone is heard and understood.

Since different generations of employees have different views, beliefs and ideas, it is crucial to understand and decipher what they need and how they need it, and then work around them to ensure open communication, a free flow of ideas, creativity, innovation and massive results.

**Bridging the Gap**

After analyzing the communication language of your current workforce on an aggregate as well as individual level, take time to review the results with your team and implement the 4 keys of communication according to their preferred communication style. Remember, there is no good or bad score. You will have your top languages as well as the ones in which you can work on.

The deviation between where you are and where you want to be is the gap that this book aims to bridge. We build better companies, have happier people, and a more satisfying world, when we learn how to speak, hear, listen and understand.

To do this, we will discuss the ethos, pathos and logos of good communication in the next chapter.

# CHAPTER 6

# Building the Bridge

PERSONAL CORE VALUE #6:

*Learn to give more than you get so any return is more than you expect.*

Learn to give more than you get so any return is more than you expect.

Bridges are meant to allow traffic to move in two directions. We get into trouble when we don't understand this principle. The solution or resolve may be headed in your direction, but you are impeding progress by insisting traffic is one way.

Over the last few chapters, we have discussed how much the workforce has changed across the generations and how it will continue to change in the future. We have also looked at ways we can understand better and become better speakers, hearers, and listeners in the workplace. In this chapter, we will learn how to bridge the communication gap that exists within our cross-generational workforce.

## Aristotle and Communication

Before we talk about bridging the gap, it is important to understand the psychological constructs needed for effective communication. To do this, we use Aristotle's Ethos, Pathos, and Logos philosophy.

**Ethos, Pathos** and **Logos** are three Greek terms coined by the philosopher, Aristotle. They represent three basic pillars of effective and persuasive communication that are often used to convince an audience. For our purposes, our audience is our employees and teams.

Before we dive into how we build the bridge, let's discuss these three terms in more detail.

**Ethos,** when translated to English, means appealing to ethics. This component of communication refers to the effort to convince your audience of your credibility, trustworthiness or character. With younger employees, just having a title that is higher in rank than theirs is not enough. You need to show them that you put in the work and have earned the title you possess. You can tap into the Ethos by being careful with your words and choosing the ones that reflect honesty, thoughtfulness, and attention to small details and gestures.

**Pathos** means appealing to emotions, feelings and sentiment. Your team members, whether they are superiors or subordinates, would be more receptive to communication when their emotions are being moved. In other words, you have to find what moves them or motivates them and communicate with them in that way. Pathos can be used in both a negative and positive manner. If someone has negative feelings about something, you can use your communication to ignite those feelings and if someone feels passionately about something you can push those buttons as well. By tapping into pathos, people's emotions can drive them to act. The general rule of thumb is to incorporate pathos in the introduction and conclusion – grab your audience's attention when communicating with them and leave them with action-oriented information that they can use.

**Logos** refers to appealing to the listener's logic. This means using logic and reason to drive your audience to act. Effective arguments used to invoke logos include testimonials, survey statistics and other supporting details to back up claims, ideas, and positions. The most common ways logos is used are through storytelling, logical arguments, facts, recorded evidence, historical data and literal analogies. Keep in mind, the information must **matter** to your employees, and must be presented in a way that they understand what you intend for them to understand.

When you use ethos, pathos and logos, you ensure your listeners understand your message, trust you as a communicator, and remember the emotions that drive them toward action. These three elements – ethos, pathos and logos reinforce each other. If you can manage to integrate all three, you can create a good foundation for efficient and persuasive communication within your organization.

### Constructing the Bridge

Let's discuss the bridge we are attempting to build here. How do we typically define a bridge?

*A bridge is a passage that connects two different end points in space and time. It can be any length or distance and can connect phases, locations, and generations.*

# Bridging the Gap

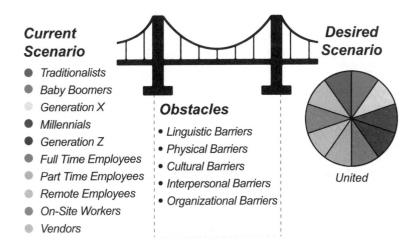

**Current Scenario**

- Traditionalists
- Baby Boomers
- Generation X
- Millennials
- Generation Z
- Full Time Employees
- Part Time Employees
- Remote Employees
- On-Site Workers
- Vendors

**Obstacles**

- Linguistic Barriers
- Physical Barriers
- Cultural Barriers
- Interpersonal Barriers
- Organizational Barriers

**Desired Scenario**

United

In this context, we are aiming to bridge the gap between the communication styles and languages of older generations with the communication styles and languages of younger generations. While both sides are right to adhere to the way that they communicate, it is important to understand our differences and how we can meet in the middle to achieve goals, break barriers, reduce turnover, and boost engagement.

Let's discuss each element individually.

**The Current Scenario**

The current scenario, as we have discussed in-depth in previous chapters, is that there are 5 generations of employees struggling to communicate in the workforce. The majority of older generations of employees follow traditional communication practices while younger generations of employees consider more modern communication styles. As a result, the reality is that employees tend

73

to work in clusters and gravitate to those of the same generation over those within a different generation. This is what tends to create a massive communication gap.

## The Desired Scenario

As you can see in the diagram above, the desired scenario talks about one united team – a synergy among employees across the different generations who pool their experiences, resources, expertise, technology, and acumen together to generate major results as a team and as an organization.

This could look like older employees mentoring their younger peers by virtue of their age and experiences. This also looks like younger employees giving insight into ways the company can serve their local community better. It helps add an incredible balance to the organization.

## Obstacles Holding Us Back

There are several obstacles or barriers standing in the way that have caused a divide between the current and desired scenarios.

Fundamentally, these barriers can be categorized into five types:

- Linguistic barriers
- Physical barriers
- Cultural barriers
- Interpersonal barriers
- Organizational barriers

As organizations undergo a global digital transformation, employees often witness certain obvious linguistical and cultural barriers that make communicating very difficult. With that said, the right spirit of embracing variety, diversity, and ease of use for technology, there is no communication problem that is too big to solve.

For example, the physical barriers could represent the way an office is designed such as with closed offices, divided cubicles, and opaque windows to conference rooms. This type of setup does not often scream that one values open communication. The organizational energy is also very important to ensuring an environment of effective communication.

Interpersonal barriers can often represent internal biases that employees may have which can cloud their communication. Organizational barriers also represent the morals, values and general mood of the organization. Paying attention to these types of obstacles and taking steps to show the organization where and how to fix them can help to bridge the communication gap.

**The Bridge**

The bridge is known as the pathway we follow to hear and listen to each other and seek to genuinely understand each other. It is how we achieve and seek to value an environment of open and authentic communication.

Open, authentic, and effective communication practices must be intentional and enforced throughout any organization in order to be able to bridge the communication gap that exists. The senior most executives must be responsible for setting this precedent and lead by example.

HR managers must also ensure the people they hire understand teams are communicating well and employees are feeling heard and valued. They must also ensure employees are well trained in the technologies used within the organization and that there are planned mentorship programs executed properly.

Creating concise communication channels and maintaining them with a respectful tone, encouraging inquisitiveness of employees and providing a wholesome learning and working experience are all key aspects in this respect. There must be a healthy blend of traditional and modern communication practices and a careful selection of communication styles to be used throughout the organization as well as between and among various divisions and teams.

## Best Practices for Building the Bridge

Now, let's discuss best practices organizations can adopt to successfully bridge the communication gap and create a unified workforce.

### A. Practices of the Older Generations to Incorporate

*This is the older generations of employees referred to as traditionalists, baby boomers and Generation X employees.*

Here are some best practices that we can learn from and incorporate into practice today, with a bit of a twist of course.

1. The human touch – Face to face meetings are a fairly regular thing. This is one of the most important things in today's digital age – keeping the human touch. However, we know that daily or regular face to face meetings can be both time consuming, and difficult in cases where global or remote teams are the norm. Therefore, organizations can have face to face meetings within offices on a bi-monthly basis, so managers and employees are able to interact with each other. It might feel a little bit old school, but it helps to keep the spark alive.

2. Mentoring – The most age old practice is that of mentoring. When the oldies were actually newbies, they would pick the manager or supervisor whose career path they wanted to follow and then take active mentorship from them. This is a golden practice that should be kept alive. As times changes, methods and practices will also change but some of the core characteristics and principles should be brought forward to

the current generation of employees. A fat paycheck isn't the only thing that will keep millennials and Gen Z employees around for long.

**B. Practices of the Younger Generations to Incorporate**

*This is the younger generations within the organization: the Millennials and Generation Z's.*

Not only do they have a digital-focused mindset, but they also have many digitally enabled practices that can help to bridge the communication gap. The ones to really hold on to are:

1. If its "textable," don't call for a meeting. Part of having an environment of open and effective communication is being direct and getting straight to the point of the conversation in many instances. Emails, text messages, and even direct messages on social media is the typical preference to communicate. This should be included within the company guidelines as much as possible as a general rule of thumb. It helps cut through the red tape, saves time on unnecessary conversations, small talk and distractions, and is conducive to a working environment for younger employees.

2. Glocal (or the concept of being both global and local) – As companies and teams continue to go global and tap into newer and more streamlined markets, the ability that this generation has of going glocal really can create an environment of open communication and give them the freedom they desire to share their ideas in any forum they choose. Younger generations love the experience that comes with working alongside other cultures, ethnicities, and even time zones.

3. Community outreach programs – The younger the generation, the more aligned they are to service and giving back to their communities, going on service trips, and organizing a cause.

This means companies must ensure they are able to pull teams together both inside the office and outside the office to work together outside to do some good in the world. This not only feels good for younger employees, but it can serve as a team building activity especially when a variety of generations are involved.

Blending all of these practices into one solid, cohesive, and serious communication strategy is the way to not only bridge this gap but to also reduce turnover, build employee engagement, create momentum, and align each member to their gifts and talents as well as the company's goals.

Managers and company executives must focus an engendering productive, company-wide communication rather than getting distracted by the endless stream of new office perks and culture trends. An out of the box work environment and culture is what can help to create a situation of open communication.

Employees cannot lead companies anymore just by virtue of their age or experience. It is the work, talent, and ability to take risks and succeed that tend to speak volumes today. If organizations and employees together do not embrace the new realities of company culture, they will not be successful in navigating the dynamics of today's business world. By embracing each employee's unique career journey and continually creating easier channels for cross-generational communication and collaboration, you can focus on what the main focus is: building a cohesive team that communicates effectively.

# CHAPTER 7

# Intentional Talk

PERSONAL CORE VALUE #7:
*Words matter!*
(my next book.)

Everyone needs to practice communication. Just think about it: we practice everything else in life. Why don't we practice speaking, listening, hearing and understanding with intentionality?

Doctors practice medicine; lawyers practice law; psychologists practice psychology; athletes practice their sport of choice. Why? Because they want to be more effective. They want to deliver their methods, protocols and activities with excellence.

Doesn't it seem logical that every professional should practice intentional communication?

One of our clients has a very large family wellness center. In the course of their day, they see many people with all kinds of joint and muscle issues – some chronic, some injurious and some maintenance. The doctor hired us to teach our Communication IQ™ process to the practitioners and support staff for the sole purpose of helping patients connect so they could relax. That was over 10 years ago. Today, that doctor has become one of our CIQ coaches.

Jennifer J. Deal, a research scientist for the Center for Creative Leadership said:

*"The so-called generation gap is, in large part, the result of miscommunication and misunderstanding, fueled by common insecurities and the desire for clout."*

We have to this point talked about how each of the generations in the workplace are different, how every employee has a different communication style and how managers can make use of the right communication language to understand the people they work with and communicate effectively.

In this chapter, I want to put aside all of the differences and let's dive in to the one basic tactic that will ensure open communication in your workplace.

## Similarities Between the Generations

We already know how each generation differs from other. Different periods in history, how we were raised or not raised, our culture and ethnic backgrounds, our belief systems alongside so many different things inform the way we think, act, and communicate. We have also entered the workforce during different revolutions, have seen different management styles and have seen local and global markets evolve in very different ways.

However, at the end of the day, many of us are just people who want to work hard, achieve our goals and contribute to our companies and our communities in a consistent and wholesome way. As leaders, many of us want to ensure better employee engagement, logical diversity and inclusion measures, and reduce turnover and improve retention. Therefore, in this section, we will put aside our differences and look at ways in which we are similar.

## Values Matter

The first and foremost point of similarity between all of the generations of employees is that values are critically important. Values matter to most members of each generation. What are some of those key values? Integrity, honesty, a good work ethic, and trustworthiness are just a few of the top values that we seek to instill in ourselves and our children and advocate for within the workplace.

As a result, organizations must have a work environment and culture that is rich in these types of values. Establishing our values or core values as many companies refer to them is important because it is something by which everyone and everything can be measured within your organization. Problems that may arise never become personal because you can always look to the values you possess and cultivate for guidance.

## Respect Without Regard for Position or Title

The second point of similarity between all of the generations we may work alongside is that irrespective of one's position in the organizational hierarchy, all people want to be respected – from the oldest to the youngest person. You can learn to effectively communicate with your boss, your peers and coworkers, and the janitor and front office receptionist equally and respectfully.

As our times continue to advance, the concept of respect becomes even more of a need and a reality. Many of the social and even political situations we encounter at a national and global scale is simply because we fail to see everyone as equal without regard for their title, position, or economic status and show equal respect across the board.

Within every organization, you can be the change agent that ensures there is a genuine basic level of respect for all employees – from the CEO to the janitor and everyone in between. To thrive in communication, it is important to create an environment where respect is not just mandated, but it exists automatically in free flowing manner.

## An Environment Built on Trust

A third point of similarity between all of the varied generations of employees is that each one wants an environment that is built on trust. It has been said that trust is hard to win and even harder to win back. Employees need to be able to trust that their managers are communicating and acting in ways that are open and authentic, that they are presenting all the information needed upfront, and not plotting political powerplays behind closed doors.

Employees also want to know that they are working with trustworthy peers. Each other's best interests should be at the heart of the other person. It's a very basic principle but it is missing from much of our workplaces. We may say that we trust each other, but do we really trust each other to not only keep our word, but act in congruence with what we say and believe?

## Honesty with Change

Let's be honest here: Change affects us all differently. When things change around us it can cause us to be uncertain and to feel unstable in our thinking and in our relationships. But change, when it is not discussed openly especially within an organization, it can cause trust to erode. Creating the trusted advisor role is more important now than ever.

Irrespective of age, position, or even experience, all employees want to be understood and heard when change is happening around them. Create an environment that allows for open discussions around changing strategies, plans, and dialogues. Let people in on the company planning for the future. Ask for their feedback and take it in to consideration as a leader who may be leading a team or an entire company.

This is especially true of millennials and Gen Z employees; they don't just go along to get along. Gen Zers need to understand why you are implementing a new policy or revising procedures. Millennials need to understand why and how it will benefit the organization and community. It is easy to think millennials are more aligned to change and adaptation, but the truth is, the struggle with change is not confined to one generation. They just tend to deal with it better. The younger generations are less likely to stay in the same place for two or three decades. They often seek out personal growth, and if they do not feel they are advancing in the company, they will likely be susceptible to poaching by competitors.

**Avoid Monotony**

One final critical similarity between all generations of employees is that monotony frustrates. Doing the same thing over and over again, day in and day out often gets old for most people. Since we spend at least half of our lives at work or working, it is important that work is made fun and something that we are motivated and excited to approach each day. For example, while older generations are motivated by loyalty and long-term job security, younger generations are motivated by a cause that is inspiring to them. They have to feel a sense of gratitude and even privilege to get up, get dressed, and get to work.

The absence of this serotonin rush can lead to reduced levels of productivity, complacent attitudes, and an unwillingness to give their best performance each day. When this is the case, it impacts other members of the team, whole teams, and even entire companies as well.

One of the best experiences in my career journey was when I was a board member of a very large non-profit organization that had a global footprint. The executive complained about staff not being engaged and poor attendance to meetings. I asked if I could host the next meeting and was given permission. I immediately sent out an email with all the necessary information.

On the day of the meeting, I had arranged for a charter bus to be waiting hidden outside. When it was time to start the meeting everyone who was on time were instructed to get on the bus, those who were late or didn't show up were left behind. Once underway, I announced to everyone we were going to the local mall for a contest. The contest was that everyone received a crisp $100 bill and once we hit the mall, they had 45 minutes to spend every cent exactly with receipts and a show and tell. If they didn't spend to the last penny the full $100, they had to return everything to the store and the $100.

Our rendezvous was a nice restaurant in the mall for lunch. Needless to say, show and tell was interesting to say the least. The result of that excursion was that no one was late or missed a staff meeting from there on.

Despite the differences, various generations of employees have many of the same very basic human traits in common. Once you understand each person's communication style which is unique and start communicating with them in that way, you can use some of these commonalities to ensure long-term and consistently effective communication.

Let's look at some ways we can do that.

## Conscious Communication

Tapping into the similarities that employees share while keeping in mind their differences is the right way to ensure effective communication in the workplace. It is a careful balance and it takes some work, but it can be done. The key is to mix drivers and needs while encouraging them to act.

Let's take for instance Thomas - a Traditionalist. If you desire to communicate well with Thomas, you must keep in mind that in general, he expects to be approached with respect. His seniority is important to him. Additionally, Thomas is keen on ensuring his work is more accurate and that he has all of the facts. A traditionalist like Thomas will likely spend his entire career with the same company.

Consider using a formal tone of communication with Thomas and the best option for a meeting would likely be one that is face to face. If the matter does not require a meeting, you may want to drop a written note on his desk over sending an email.

Now, let's take Bertha as an example. Bertha is a Baby Boomer. You know she is a workaholic and demands very high quality of work of herself and her team. She also has a high level of team spirit and will almost always be available for a quick chat. She would like for you to just stop in on a whim in her office every once in a while, to tell her how your day is going or to ask her a question but more than likely she'd prefer if you talk about your work.

Being a workaholic, she isn't one for too much small talk. So, remember to get to the point as soon as possible and to be crisp in your communication. Consider a semi-formal tone and remember, she isn't one to shy away from questioning authority either.

If something bothers you, she would like to hear about it and will work to see about a mutual solution.

If we remember from the previous chapter, every person on our team can speak all seven languages at one time or another, however a generational perspective layered on top of those languages can give an accent and imply a different understanding. Take for example, being born and raised in the United States and speaking English as a native language is much different than someone who has emigrated to the United States from Mexico and learns to speak English as a second language. While the full conversation may be in English, the dialect is different and can imply a variety of meanings. The same is true of conversations between the different generations. Older and younger generations can be talking to each other, but each party is filtering what the other has said through their communication language.

Now, if you were to talk to Xavier – a Generation X employee, consider starting by asking how they are doing or how their day is going. They are a bit more personal, but one or two questions are enough. Don't go overboard or they will feel like you are preparing them for something. Xavier would likely not mind levelling with you so that you can feel free to share any idea with him.

Even though Xavier does enjoy the occasional meeting, if it is not that big of a deal, it's better to just drop him an email. He has a schedule for checking and answering emails each day and chances are he doesn't go through his phone or social media messages that often while at work. A Gen X employee like Xavier will definitely enjoy getting feedback on his projects or discussing the collaborative nature of the work environment. Additionally, he will likely allow you the autonomy to do things your way if he thinks you are capable of making good decisions and accomplishing the task well.

Now, let's move to Michelle, the consummate millennial. Michelle is focused on moving the ball forward and being aware of what is trending or new in her industry. She likely wants to do something with whatever new information she finds and prefers to be the first to get there.

Extremely driven and passionate, Michelle most likely does not like to waste a second of her time. Consider sending her text messages over email or phone calls. Try to avoid irrelevant pleasantries, small talk and keep your messages brief to initiate the conversation. A millennial like Michelle likes the back and forth quick dialogue and may include an emoji or two during the course of the conversation.

If you are a manager of a millennial, be sure that she is given work that has more meaning to her than just being a simple 9-5 desk job. Tap into her creativity and resourcefulness and make sure you bring out the best in her. If you are a millennial manager, be sure to do the same for members on your team. You can relate to each other and can use it as a tool of efficiency to get work done in the best way possible.

Zoey is a Generation Z employee. She may be new to the role or the field and is likely still exploring her options. However, if you are a manager of Zoey, know that while she may be young, she does have a lot of ideas to bring to the table. Therefore, consider giving her work that isn't routine, allow her to experiment with different teams and help her to discover and cultivate what she thinks would be the best fit for her. Let her user her technological acumen to push forward to doing the best job she can do and being the best employee she can be.

Understanding what each generation wants and how you can give it to them is key to ensuring there is a culture of effective communication and freedom to express ideas within the workplace.

## Intentionally Starting the Conversation

While each generation has specific communication styles and languages, knowing their preferred method is just the start of developing a great intergenerational relationship in the workplace. To pave the way, make sure you start with sincere intentionality. It will take work to get there especially if this is not already your company's culture.

Encourage supervisors, team leaders, managers, and executives to have a communicative environment. It doesn't mean there is a free for all. It does mean that people feel there is space to talk and be heard and understood. Making a conscious effort intentionally and initially will soon allow these types of conversations to grow organically and help your company gain a reputation for high employee engagement and retention. When the leaders of a company or team lead the way, it sets the bar of expectation for everyone else.

## The Real Barrier

As millennials take on more leadership roles and Generation Z enters the workforce, Baby Boomers and Generation X employees are faced with the huge challenge of effectively communicating with their younger team members. Miscommunication or errors in communication within the workplace could cost the business a lot. A Holmes Report study revealed that the total cost of employee misunderstanding rose to $37 billion, with an average cost per company of $62.4 million. So now, it isn't just about the work environment and culture, it is also about the company's bottom line.

The real barrier between the older and younger generations communicating openly is that we spend less time seeking to understand each other. The time period in which each generation was raised owe a lot to this difference in understand. Baby Boomers and Gen X were raised at a time of economic tension and some have experienced the struggle to survive. Millennials, on the other hand, were raised in more stable times and likely had a lot more technology incorporated into their upbringing.

If this is the case, older generations value compensation, health benefits and job security much more than their job-hopping counterparts. This is definitely not the case with younger generations. Since many Millennials had access to technology growing up, it helped them to learn and understand how to manage and work in a world that is constantly changing. They also witnessed the business world change completely, as things moved from 9-5 to the gig economy, typical office culture to remote teams and expanding globally to going glocal.

These types of changes are deeply rooted and inherent differences that cannot be overlooked. Communicating intentionally also means being willing to check certain boxes. When millennial Mike receives a text message from his boss, he might be more likely to reply to it outside of the 9-5 work hours. But when Baby Boomer Bonnie calls for an all-team meeting in-office first thing in the morning, the younger members of her team might dread the idea. Beyond technology and communication styles, languages have evolved as well. Consider, the abbreviated language styles that are used today: BRB *(Be Right Back)*, BYOD *(Bring Your Own Device)*, OOO *(Out of Office)*, IKR *(I Know Right)*. Your traditionalist manager may have a difficult time hearing what you said.

With these types of barriers, it becomes more and more important to INTENTIONALLY initiate communication changes. While this may seem like a quick and easy task, it is very much achievable and worth achieving. Millennials are eager to learn and enjoy discovering the "why" behind things. Teamwork is important to them and are more likely to build something amazing when they have a supportive team around them.

Only with intentional talk, intentional understanding, intentional communication and a conscious effort to create a work environment and culture that enables open communication can a truly united and efficient workforce within an organization be created, bought into and thrive.

# CHAPTER 8

# Intentional Response

PERSONAL CORE VALUE #8:
*Measure twice,
cut once!*

This saying is usually reserved for carpenters, but I have borrowed it for the way I choose to respond in any given situation. I find it much easier to build relationship equity if I measure my response twice before choosing the best way to shape the conversation. Don't let your mouth sabotage your intentions.

> *"Only two things are infinite, the universe and human stupidity...
> and I'm not sure about the former."*
> —*Albert Einstein*

*"OK, Boomer!"*

*"OK, Zoomer!"*

In case you have not heard these phrases, these are two of the most common comebacks in the workplace.

"OK, Boomer!" represents every millennial eye roll when a baby boomer behaves in a typical boomer manner. "OK, Zoomer!" is typically how boomers respond to millennials when they are doing something that would typically be classified as a very millennial thing to do.

In almost every work environment, ego clashes turn into frustrating communication barriers as older generations hold tightly to experience and younger generations hold tightly to the strong winds of change. This all induces a needed shift in the way we not only communicate with each other by speaking, but also in the way we choose to respond to situations, questions, attitudes, and behaviors we encounter.

## The Shift

Pew Research noted in a report that Millennials will soon be the largest living generation in the United States labor force. Generation Z currently constitutes 5% of the U.S. labor force. As numbers like these continue to grow, the shift becomes even more inevitable.

What exactly is the shift?

The shift here refers to the ways in which we respond to each other. Enough with the "OK, Boomer!" and "OK, Zoomer!" comebacks. We must work to ensure all of our employees and team members know and feel that our responses to them are equal and respectful, regardless of position, seniority or varying perspectives. Ensuring everyone is on the same page with regard to the plans and objectives of the company is not an easy task but it is a manageable one. While we do speak all of the seven languages: Mover, Doer, Influencer, Shaper, Producer, Contemplator, and Responder – our perspectives and perceptions are very different depending on the situation, but they can also be equally the same at times.

## Understanding How They Think

Before we can bridge the communication gap between older and newer generations of employees, it is absolutely important that you understand the way each of them think. This table will help you understand the basis on which we interpret a situation and form a response.

| Perceptions: | Behavior in the workplace | Leadership Style | Making decisions | Official communication style |
|---|---|---|---|---|
| Traditionalists | Usually are sticklers for rules, respect and hierarchy; are very "by the book" in their approach | Expects to exercise control over the team | They will seek approval before taking a decision | They tend to follow the top down |
| Baby Boomers | Challenged existing rules and attempt to change the status quo; true believers in mentorship and training | Often has a unilateral leadership approach | They take a decision and then inform their teams | They are usually very guarded and speak only when needed |
| Generation X | Recreated all the rules and disrupted the status quo; prefer to learn independently | Believe in coaching and guiding their teams | They include the team in exploring options, but the final decision is a solo call | They would normally make their own intelligences and stick around to those |
| Millennials | Established new rules for the new world of work; believe in personal growth and collaborative approaches to solving problems | Firm believers in teamwork and a collaborative approach | The team takes the decision unanimously | Fact based and research backed decision making in teams |
| Generation Z | Created a workplace that is an adequate mix of digital and human touches; believe they can learn anything, anytime, and anywhere; often seek growth opportunities | Wants continuous feedback and a collaborative approach | Fact based and research backed decision making in teams | Quick, seamless, diverse and inclusive |

This table can help you to understand how each generation thinks, perceives, and decides to take action. Once you understand these fundamentals behind each response, you can better understand how to make sure you are communicating effectively with them. Apart from that, you can make use of a few other tactics to gain a positive response. These are:`

- **Listen intently and actively:** A response such as "OK, Boomer!" or "OK, Zoomer!" means the other side has already had enough of the conversation. We discover more and gain back their attention by asking questions, listening to what is said, and engaging the discussion with their point of view. It is important to develop active listening habits so that we hear what is being said. Listening, hearing and truly understanding are the key to effective conversations that have meaning and that lead to thought or action.

- **Show respect regardless of position, role, or title:** Respect today isn't revered like it was in previous decades. Many of us operate with the idea that if you show me respect, I will show you respect as a favor. More so now than ever, respect doesn't just happen; it has to be earned. Respect is earned by building trust and spending time with others. Older employees must let go of their habit of commanding respect and start taking steps to earn it.

- **Focus on more than just making money:** Younger generations love a nice paycheck, but more than that, want to know that there work matters. They want to inspire change, create change and be part of any type of revolution that is focused on a cause. This is certainly something that won't hurt older generations to incorporate in processes and opportunities. Different perspectives can prove to be very powerful in chang-

95

ing not just the way teams work, but also the image and even reputation of the company.

- **Deliver what you promise:** Many organizations struggle because they often over promise and under deliver. Instead of talking about the kind of work environment and office culture you have, let employees reflect it in the type of work they do, how they communicate with customers, and how they discover solutions to problems. HR managers must roll up their sleeves and work hard to deliver on the kind of environment they imagine and, in many cases, have promised.

- **Be authentic:** There is been a long standing myth that, "The best way to address generational issues is to show there aren't any." While this may have worked before, it doesn't really work anymore. Instead, the best way to address generational issues is to acknowledge them, understand them and actively work to make them better.

- **Stay current:** As the workforce moves more rapidly from physical offices and cubicles to a remote, work from home environment, it is important to ensure your workplace is shifting effectively with the current times. While some are sticking to physical offices, be sure to put some time into creating an open space concept that makes room for collaboration and sharing of ideas. If you are moving to more of a remote focused workplace, engage your employees on the process, ask them questions and for solutions to how to make the process better. Business as usual is no longer business as usual, but business accelerated.

### Making It Work

As we have established, the best way to make a multi-generational workforce work is to acknowledge the needs of the various employees and to embrace the differences that exist. If we desire to truly achieve meaningful and authentic communication within our work environments, every generation is important and must play its part.

So how do we create this bridge and fearlessly cross it? Here are some practical thoughts for managers and leaders in the Traditionalist, Baby Boomer and Generation X categories:

- Respect the millennial and Generation Z team members. Embrace their way of communicating and working. Replace making assumptions with asking questions. Rather than leaving them out of discussions, choose to stimulate their thinking. Meaningful conversations with younger employees may also help you to uncover new learnings as well.

- Be open to contributions and ideas from your younger peers. Create a place at the table for them. Take time to learn from them about new technologies and trends to help lessen the proverbial digital divide. Make an effort to speak the digital language which in turn will make conversations more meaningful.

- Though older employees typically prefer in-person, telephone or even e-mail conversations, take time to understand that some ways of communication have changed and the leverage that is given to some of these newer forms. For your younger team members, a text message will be received with just as much as importance as a face to face conversation would be.

- Extend more autonomy and trust to the younger team members. Give them the opportunity to succeed, to fail, to make mistakes, and to create and think about solutions to problems that have never been done that way before.

- Boomers are very competitive and often tend to disregard their own emotional well-being, which influences the emotional well-being of younger generations at work. More face to face communication opportunities should be created between the different generations to raise awareness of emotions such as empathy and kindness.

While these steps can help to build the bridge from the top down, it is important to have equal movement from the other side to meet in the middle. Millennials and Generation Z can also take action to help foster a truly collaborative and open workplace.

- Develop and display empathy and support toward your older peers and leaders. Their unfamiliarity with digital communication and newer technologies could be just as frustrating to them as their lack of understanding is to you. Take into consideration their preferences for in-person communication and be patient and humble when sharing your expertise with them.

- Although you likely have a high level of confidence, resilience, and stand firmly behind what you believe, it is important that you have an open mind and approach relationships with older employees in a positive way. Actively seek out their thoughts and embrace their guidance and advice, as age does bring along some wonderful experience.

- Make a conscious effort to pursue a healthy work-life balance. Retain your ability and mentality around travel, vacations, weekend getaways, and general fun in life. It can not only lighten up an entire office but assist those around you in reviewing their work-life balance. Boomers have historically neglected their personal well-being and family commitments to make successful careers amid harsh competition. As times change, this will change also.

The challenge with meaningful conversations behind office doors, cubicles, emails, and often phone calls is that responses are either not conveyed well or are not received well. Ultimately, if we are to bridge the gap, we must make sure that this divide is narrowed down. The ego clash must come to an end, and employees must understand their own and each other's communication style to respond correctly for effective communication to take place.

It is well understood that both older and younger generations require the human element – the only difference is in the degree to which it is preferred. This is where we both can work together, meet halfway and then strive to take it forward.

# CHAPTER 9

# What a Communication Map Can Tell You

Find out where the skunks live and don't try to out stink them.

When pressure is applied to something, whatever is inside is coming out, so in the process of creating communication pathways, unintended consequences such as the exposure of character, or the revealing of attitudes come squirting out and may not smell very good.

This is one reason CIQ communication mapping is important. It tells us where the skunks live so we can prepare a proper greeting.

Communication is a two-way street with many stops in between. How do we connect our ability to listen, speak, hear and understand? We do that with the help of a communication map. Creating a communication map helps to aid the company's internal communications process. And, as a side note, it also can form a foundation for communicating at home, at school, and in other everyday social interactions.

A communication map is what can be used throughout your organization to navigate through the hierarchy, communicate information well and make the workflow of a project or task more nimble, agile, and decisive. The main objective with this communication map is to ensure seamless and effective cross-generational communication.

The basis of this communication map will be the 7 communication languages or communication styles we learned about in previous chapters. For purposes of recall, these are:

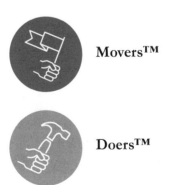

**Movers™**

**Doers™**

**Influencers™**

 **Responders™**

 **Shaper™**

 **Producers™**

 **Contemplators™**

However, one very important feature of all of these languages is that every individual possesses all 7. There is no one size fits all. Rather, multiple sizes fit for different situations at different times and around different people. When two people communicate, they try to gauge the dominant communication style of the other and respond in an effective manner. This gauging can be done by understand the "CrossTalks Index" – a term coined in the book *Communication IQ*™.

## CrossTalks Index

CrossTalks refer to the convergence of two or more communication styles between two or more individuals. Since every individual possesses all seven languages in varying degrees, the similar the variations, the fewer CrossTalks; the more different these variations are, the higher the CrossTalks will be.

You will often see that people who are similar in the way they think, behave and speak get along in understanding each other quite well, whereas chaos, frustration or misunderstanding may ensue when two polar opposites attempt to communicate. This is because polar opposite personalities have very high variations in their language degrees. Obviously, there are pros and cons of being very similar or very different, but as a manager or leader within your company, the goal is never to change anybody but to ensure there is healthy and open communication between all employees and teams and everyone feels heard and valued.

It is critical to also understand that a low or high score in any of these languages does not determine the effectiveness of an employee. These scores only help in understanding how teams can be formed in a way where there isn't fighting or hurt feelings as a result. This does not mean grouping together all the people who are alike, as that will kill creativity and set a monotonous tone to the environment. Instead, managers must keep a healthy mix of all the languages on each team so that there is always a unanimous decision but an informed one.

The CrossTalks Index becomes more and more important today as companies grow exponentially and become increasingly global – thereby having employees from different cultures, age intelligences, backgrounds and countries work on the same teams and rely on each other to produce great work. This index provides the foundation towards creating a unified workforce in a multi-generational environment.

Another part of the seven communication styles is that they can be grouped into three overarching categories.

## The 3 Intelligences

Predominantly, all seven languages can be divided into three intelligences: **Kinetic**, **Emotive** and **Cognitive**.

The **Kinetic** intelligences includes **Movers** and **Doers**. These intelligences include those individuals who are very creative, robust, responsive and believe in getting things done. Action oriented, loyal and highly pragmatic, they tend to always finish what they start. As the name suggests, they are all about constantly moving the ball forward and ensuring things get done and the company grows.

The **Emotive** intelligence comprises **Responders** and **Influencers**. They are very passionate, emphatic, warm, people-oriented and enthusiastic individuals who love to influence and network. They are usually the ones who set the tone and environment within the workplace. They are called Emotive as they tend to set the emotional tone for the office and for the people.

The last intelligence is the **Cognitive** intelligence. This intelligence is comprised of **Shapers**, **Contemplators** and **Producers**, and is named so as it involves those who focus on the why behind things. The direction of thought tends to push them to make decisions when they have gathered all the pertinent information. These people tend to look at the long term goals and create and communicate a vision for the company to follow, gather resources and inculcate curiosity and a desire for their employees to carefully manage their own lives and projects.

Each of these intelligences play a vital role in ensuring a seamless and effective flow of communication within the organization. Together, they come together and help create the communication wheel. But before, we understand what a communication wheel is, we need to understand the distress levels for each of these languages.

**Distress Levels**

Distress levels refer to the various ways in which each of the 7 communication language can potentially sabotage their personal and professional lives. These differ for each person and can cause various levels of distress in their lives. Here we classify the distress levels as 1, 2 and 3 with 1 being the initial level of distress and 3 being high levels of distress.

Let us now discuss the various factors for each of them:

**Movers** – As we have already discussed Movers represent highly interactive, innovative and motivated employees. If you see them being overly demanding of themselves or their teams, very critical about every move, playing the blame game or attempting to control every action taken by the team, take these as early signs of distress. If they start becoming resentful and contemptuous understand that their distress levels have increased. And if you see them behaving in a hostile, abusive or bitter manner it could mean they are extremely distressed.

**Doers** – Early distress signals for Movers and Doers are the same, as they both belong to the Kinetic intelligence. High levels of distress for Doers can be interpreted when you see them over-extending themselves, being very critical and behaving in a self-martyring manner. When they reach the point of self-pity, resentment and abusing their teams or holding spite, it is important to understand that they are extremely distressed.

**Influencers** – If you see Influencers on your team exaggerating circumstances, being manipulative, obnoxiously optimistic or talking a lot, they are undergoing early distress symptoms. These levels become high when they start blaming others or become defensive. These levels become extreme when you see them start feeling rejected, trapped, resentful and shying away from situations.

**Responders** – Since Influencers and Responders both belong to the Emotive family, their basic distress symptoms are the same. Highly distressed Responders are often confused, make mistakes, live in a state of denial or often over explain their decisions to convince the people around them. Extremely distressed Responders loathe themselves and may even be depressed.

**Shapers** – Early indications of distress for Shapers include over or under delegation, high expectations or internal motivation and cold or indifferent behavior. Distressed Shapers start using people for their advantage, become very sarcastic, overly critical and calloused. Highly distressed Shapers tend to start withdrawing from the environment, stop trusting their teams and peers and tend to get addicted to exercise or stimulants.

**Producers** – Distressed Producers can be identified when you start seeing them become materialistic, controlling and tend to circumvent people and their ideas in order to get things done. These levels are high if they become stingy, selfish or proud, and extreme when they start to withdraw from the environment, hoard value and are emotionally abusive.

**Contemplators** – Slightly distressed Contemplators have a low self-confidence, withdrawal symptoms and are proud and critical. When highly distressed, they live in denial and become defensive, inflexible and legalistic. Extremely distressed Contemplators become more withdrawn, critical and often feel rejected or used.

These distress levels when emerging at an individual level tend to seep through the organization and disrupt communication flow and workflow, thus affecting the work environment and the company's progress, productivity and growth. Therefore, it is important to keep a check on what traits to foster, what traits to flag and manage, and how to control the flow of communication within the workplace. This can be done by using a communication wheel.

## The Communication Wheel

The communication wheel refers to the cycle of communication that should ideally be followed in an organization. The cycle has been broken down into seven steps, clearly defining the role of each language, traits to foster and traits to flag.

This breakdown has been done to ensure a better understanding of the wheel – but keep in mind that this is an ongoing cycle that helps ensure a seamless and effective flow of communication at your workplace. It may be necessary to come back to parts of this wheel for understanding and reinforcements.

We begin the process with the **Emotive** category.

**Step 1:** Responders™

Responders begin the communication cycle. As they receive the company's goals, objectives, strategies, plans and targets, it is their job to initiate the transfer of this information throughout the organization. Here, managers must ensure that they tap into their compassion, passion and creativity while keeping an eye out for symptoms of distress such as complaining, being offensive or even depressed.

**Step 2:** Influencers™

Influencers help take the communication forward by creating a hype around them and making sure everyone on the team is excited, motivated and focused. Managers must make good use of their intuition, inclusivity and zest to carry the flow of communication forward but must watch out for distress signals such as denial, argumentativeness or withdrawal.

Once the Emotive category of individuals have successfully set the tone for the workplace, we then move to the **Cognitive** category of individuals to take the wheel further.

**Step 3:** Shapers™

Managers and company leaders tend to be shapers and come to other shapers on their team for their organization skills, strategic thinking and focus to take the vision forward. They must, however, make sure that Shapers aren't overly critical of members of their team or their ideas, eliminating goals or necessary steps to reach the goals, or taking over the process entirely.

**Step 4:** Producers™

It is now time for Producers to start the flow of work with optimum allocation of resources. Managers must take advantage of their financial adeptness, hospitality and resourcefulness to get the right things, right people and right tasks at the right place and the right time. They must watch out for symptoms such as over-organizing to the point of obsession, becoming restrictive or miserly with the resources.

**Step 5:** Contemplators™

It is now time for the Contemplators to use their intelligence, inquisitiveness and philosophies to drive the vision, goals and strategies of the organization forward. They think about the big picture from all angles and will come back within some time to give their opinion. However, managers must intervene if they see them over justify, accuse others or show withdrawal symptoms.

The individuals in the Cognitive category play their part in making sure everyone is on the same page about what to do and is motivated and driven to get what has been agreed to done. Following this, the **Kinetic** intelligence of individuals start actually initiating the work.

**Step 6: Doers™**

Nothing sets the tone better than actually taking action to get things done. Here, Doers set the tone with their pragmatism, diligence and focused way of getting things done and bringing things to fruition. They can, however, get toxic if they start playing the blame game, grumbling or self-martyring especially when projects get stalled or are not going in the way they have planned. Thus managers need to watch out for those signals.

**Step 7: Movers™**

Action in the right direction is what helps organizations achieve goals and grow. It is what often sets good companies apart from great companies. This direction is guided by Movers, as they are extremely innovative, straightforward and always set the bar high. However, if they start getting demanding or offensive, managers must intervene.

As a leader within your organization, you must ensure this flow is followed optimally. Pay attention to the good traits and foster them but pay extra attention to distress signals and take care of them before they escalate or spread within the organizational hierarchy.

All of this helps in plotting the coordinates of the communication map, which is followed by every organization. This results in what is known as "Relationship Equity" throughout the various levels of the organization. We'll discuss more on how to create relationship equity in the next chapter.

# CHAPTER 10

# Relationship Equity

PERSONAL CORE VALUE #10:

*Never stop making relationship deposits even when it's hard or you see it as a waste of time.*

It's always hard for me to believe that someone may not like me or not want to get along with me. After all, I'm wonderful! The sad truth is that there are apparently some people who may not put me on their trusted advisor list just yet.

One of the things that the CIQ system has substantially advanced in my effort to be an intentional communicator is to never burn bridges in front of anyone. Keep making relationship deposits because you never know when you may need to make a withdrawal or an advance or they may need a withdrawal or advance.

Situations and circumstances are in constant flux these days. Sometimes, it is in no small measure that our success is a result of careful and legitimate relationship deposits.

You have now made it this far in the book. You have gained a better understanding of how the modern work environment has evolved over the past few decades. You also understand the current situation of how we tend to communicate and even miscommunicate with each other. Now, you know what an ideal communication situation looks like, understand our unique human similarities and differences, and how to bridge the gap to drive forward a sustained impact. The one thing remaining is how all of this talk around communication collectively impacts your organization.

Obviously, all of this hard work and hassle has got to be worth the tassel. What is your reward? Why should open and effective communication matter within your organization? How does it impact overall growth and the bottom line? The answer is found in *Relationship Equity*.

In this chapter, we are going to discuss the importance of building relationship equity and the impact that it can have throughout your organization.

**Why the Hard Work?**

You have likely put hours upon hours, thousands and thousands of dollars and multiple resources into training, developing and coaching your employees and equipping them with the best tools to be successful in their jobs. However, all of this could be for naught if they cannot work together and communicate well to drive the goals of the organization forward. For most, the primary objective of running a business is to have a stellar top and bottom line. But in order to achieve this, the top and bottom lines must include a healthy work culture that fosters the three C's – **Connection, Communication** and **Collaboration.**

## Connection

Interpersonal connections in the workplace are essential to the attainment of organizational goals, as well as creating a unified workforce and a culture of open and free communication. At the end of the day, a team that works together becomes successful together. Therefore, as a leader, you must actively embark upon the pursuit of connection within and throughout your organization.

## Communication

While this has already been discussed at great length throughout the course of the previous 9 chapters, if I had to summarize the importance of communication in one short sentence, I would say that a team that can understand each other and communicate well functions at a significantly higher and more productive rate than the team that doesn't.

## Collaboration

An organization that successfully achieves connection and communication automatically begins to foster an environment where employees can communicate openly. This open expression of ideas leads to a truly collaborative work environment and culture.

Employing the Communication Success Wheel well and understanding the prevalent communication languages in your workforce are key to achieving these 3 C's – the elements that make up relationship equity.

**Relationship Equity**

Once you have attained connection, communication and collaboration, what you have is essentially relationship equity. Let's break this down further.

The word "relationship" means *the way in which two or more people or things are connected, or the state of being connected.* Here, we can think about the relationships that managers build with their employees and one peer builds with another peer over time.

The word "equity" means *the value* that is associated with the object of concern, which refers to the overall employee relationship.

Putting these together, "relationship equity" refers to *the value that is derived to form the relationship employees share with one another.*

The concept of relationship equity can be summed up as:

RE = *Relationship* + *Equity* + *Trust*

Where, RE = Relationship Equity

*Relationship* = Trust x Time

*Equity* = Relationship x Value

*Trust* = Connection x Authenticity

When trust is built over a period of time, relationships begin to evolve and when value is consistently added to each person's life by the other person, a long-term connection is created that often results in authentic communication. The stronger the relationship and the more value that is added over time, the more equity you will develop. It is like a house, the more money you put into it, the more equity you will have.

There are times in which we can underestimate the importance of relationships and how trust, time, connection, authenticity and value play into making those relationships better or worse.

It has been said that trust is the hardest thing to build but one of the easiest things to lose. And that is one of the reasons it is so important to not only build trust but to maintain trust. The more time you spend with someone and the more intentionality you bring to the relationship, walls are replaced by bridges and long-term value and connection is the result.

In the real world, this equity translates into the top line impacting some of the intangibles such as a culture of open communication, collaboration and a unified team effort – all of which lead to more revenue, growth and success.

But there is a catch – as the time increases, this equation doesn't just advance in summations, but exponentially. This means that the relationship equity may double, triple or even quadruple over time.

## Why Relationship Equity?

Just like generating equity on your property or in your stocks, putting in intentional effort towards building relationship equity will result in massive returns for your business. There are many advantages to intentionally building relationship equity within your organization.

Here are just a few of those:

- **Opening up of opportunities** – When your employees and teams are able to communicate openly and freely, there is a free flow of ideas, creativity and innovation. As mentioned previously, you never know where your next multi-million dollar idea can come from! This kind of communication flow can open up many opportunities for the organization.

- **Organizational harmony** – When there is trust and open communication prevalent in the organization, all five generations of employees can co-exist and collaborate harmoniously.

This leads to discipline and a high level of productivity and progress within the organization.

- **High levels of employee engagement** – When employees enjoy being at work, are unified toward the same set of goals, and when they feel valued, heard and understood, they tend to put in more work and dedication for the organization. In addition to that, work-life balance increases and extreme stress levels decrease. This leads to unprecedented levels of employee engagement.

- **Lower attrition rates** – High levels of engagement means employees would tend to stay with the organization, and as a result the retention rate would go up. This is particularly true for Millennials and Generation Z employees, as it is both meaningful work and a progressive and inclusive work environment that tends to keep them around and going.

- **Attracting better talent** – When your employees are in tune with the culture and environment you have created, they are excited to get to work and to share open roles with their friends or past colleagues who might be looking for work. If this is the case, word spreads and leads to the creation of a wonderful employer branding and having this can help to attract better talent as the organization grows.

- **Organizational growth** – When your work environment achieves and possesses both breadth and depth, it retains employees and draws top talent. This makes your company competitive and favorably impacts its bottom line. This effect crawls up throughout the organization, impacting the top line and leading to organizational growth.

With so many amazing benefits, who would not want to achieve high levels of relationship equity within their organization?

## Not All in a Day's Work

While this book discusses a number of ways in which you can improve communication in the workplace, there are a few things that you can keep in mind.

- **It is a long game** – If building and maintaining an open and collaborative communication culture at work was easy, this would not be such a major concern among managers. Therefore, you have to keep in mind that getting there is a marathon and not a sprint. Making an intentional effort one day or having everyone take their CIQ profile only will not cause everything to just magically fall into place. Every step you take in this direction is a building block and will get you to the ultimate goal of long-term relationship equity. Also, you cannot force your employees to get on board from the start. Maybe you can start with yourself and then with your team while allowing others in the organization to see the transformation.

- **Focus on your part** – When managers focus on their part of the deal, that is, being open to their seniors and peers, they set the right tone for everyone else. Listen, connect, engage, share, and over time, you will find that you have more and more relationship equity. Others get inspired and want to reciprocate equally or greater, reinforcing the growth of the relationship equity value.

## Parting Thoughts

If you are going to navigate your organization through the dynamics of today's evolving business world successfully, you need to pay attention to the pressing points – the weak nerves. One of the biggest pain points in your organization is the multi-generational demography of your employees that comes with its own set of challenges. The most sustainable way to handle this is by intentionally creating an environment that encourages open communication throughout the organization.

Open communication allows your employees to be more engaged, feel valued and heard. It helps to ensure a truly collaborative workplace, ensuring everyone clearly sees the big picture and the details as well as the part they play in its attainment. Every employee no matter where they land in the five current generations will find that effective communication keeps everyone on the same page and moving in the same direction. It leads to:

- Reduced stress

- Greater job satisfaction

- A boost in productivity

- Higher retention

- Better team building

- Increased commitment and loyalty

- Mutual respect throughout the organization.

As one of the immediate next steps, I would invite you to take the CIQ assessment. You will find a link that you can scan to access it in the back of this book. Once you have taken the assessment and understand your results, followed the principles and action points provided in this book to understand the generational gap that exists, make listening, hearing, speaking and understanding intentional practices to bridge the multi-generational gap. Attempt to eliminate negative or ego driven responses and create a workplace that thrives on mutual respect and trust. Implement the Communication Success Wheel to set the right tone, and make sure to keep an eye out for those distress signals – we all have them.

When you are happy at work, you feel happy, purposeful and driven in your personal life. This carries forward into your home, your school, your marriage, your family, your church and your community and can truly enrich your life in a meaningful and positive way. Every action, reaction and spoken or unspoken word can either build and impact your life and those around you in a meaningful level or can keep you teetering on the brink of effectiveness and progress.

Let's enrich both our professional and personal lives by making an intentional effort to communicate well.

# Appendix A

Communication IQ™ Consultants are ready to help you act, feel and think your way through the process of maximum ROII (Return on Individual Investment)

Contact our National Headquarters at:

Communication IQ™

Life Languages International™

2711 Valley View Lane Suite 103

Dallas Texas 75234

972-406-1313

To invite Gerald for a speaking engagement contact Gerald@lifelangauges.com

If you would like to become a CIQ Consultant please visit www.CommunicationIQ.US

# Take the Communication IQ™ Profile by scanning the code below with your phone

# Notes and References

## Chapter 1

Knight, Rebecca. *Managing People from 5 Generations.* 12 Aug. 2015, hbr. org/2014/09/managing-people-from-5-generations.

Svensson, Göran. "'Glocalization' of Business Activities: a 'Glocal Strategy' Approach." *Management Decision*, MCB UP Ltd, 1 Feb. 2001, www.emerald.com/insight/content/doi/10.1108/EUM0000000005403/full/html.

"Deloitte Global Millennial Survey 2020." *Deloitte*, 23 Sept. 2020, www2.deloitte.com/global/en/pages/about-deloitte/articles/millennialsurvey.html.

Fry, Richard. "Millennials Are Largest Generation in the U.S. Labor Force." *Pew Research Center*, Pew Research Center, 27 July 2020, www.pewresearch.org/fact-tank/2018/04/11/millennials-largest-generation-us-labor-force/.

Hill, Catey. "Millennials Engage with Their Smartphones More than They Do Actual Humans." *MarketWatch*, MarketWatch, 21 June 2016, www.marketwatch.com/story/millennials-engage-with-their-smartphones-more-than-they-do-actual-humans-2016-06-21.

Hassell, David. "Infographic: How Important Is Communication to Millennials?" *15Five*, 28 Feb. 2020, www.15five.com/blog/employee-communication-millennials/.

Wieczner, Jen. "10 Things Generation Y Won't Tell You." *MarketWatch*, MarketWatch, 21 Aug. 2013, www.marketwatch.com/story/10-things-millennials-wont-tell-you-2013-06-21.

## Chapter 2

"2019 Workplace Report." *15Five*, 20 Nov. 2019, www.15five.com/2019-workplace-report/.

Workplace, Quantum. *6 Insights on Effective Workplace Communication, Fierce Conversations, and Miscommunication*, 2017, www.quantumworkplace.com/fierce-conversations-effective-workplace-communication-miscommunication.

## Chapter 3

Murlis, Helen, and Peggy Schubert. "Engage Employees and Boost Performance." Hay Intelligence Inc., 2001.

Posted February 6, 2019 by NDMU | Communication. "The Evolution of Communication from Boomers to Gen Z." *NDMU Online*, 6 Feb. 2019, online.ndm.edu/news/communication/evolution-of-communication/.

Campiere, Angela. "How Generation Z Communicates at Work: Ryan Jenkins, Others Weigh IN." *PCMA*, 8 Aug. 2019, www.pcma.org/how-generation-z-communicates-work/.

Jenkins, Ryan. "This Is How Generation Z Will Communicate at Work." *Inc.com*, Inc., 8 Nov. 2017, www.inc.com/ryan-jenkins/72-percent-of-generation-z-want-this-communication-at-work.html.

## Chapter 4

Pryce-Jones, Jessica. *Happiness at Work: Maximizing Your Psychological Capital for Success*. Wiley-Blackwell, 2010.

## Chapter 5

"11 Reasons Why Business Communication Is Critical to Your Company's Success." *The Employee Communications and Advocacy Blog*, 2020, blog.smarp.com/11-reasons-why-business-communication-is-crucial-for-companys-success.

Challen, Fiona. "4 Tips to Improve Employee Communication in the Workplace." *Activate Your Employees on Social Media - Tribal Impact,*

Tribal Impact, 28 May 2020, www.tribalimpact.com/blog/how-to-improve-employee-communication-in-the-workplace.

"10 Shocking Internal Communications Stats You Can't Ignore." *The Employee Communications and Advocacy Blog*, 2020, blog.smarp.com/10-shocking-internal-communications-stats-you-cant-ignore.

Chui, Michael, et al. "The Social Economy: Unlocking Value and Productivity through Social Technologies." *McKinsey & Company*, McKinsey & Company, 13 Feb. 2019, www.mckinsey.com/industries/technology-media-and-telecommunications/our-insights/the-social-economy.

Bambost, Bart Van. "Why Internal Communication Is the Key Driver for Employee Engagement." *ThinkTalent*, 14 Feb. 2019, thinktalent.eu/why-internal-communication-is-the-key-driver-for-employee-engagement/.

## Chapter 7

AMA. "The Myth of Generational Differences in the Workplace." *American Management Association*, 24 Jan. 2019, www.amanet.org/articles/the-myth-of-generational-differences-in-the-workplace/.

Holmes Report. "The Cost of Poor Communications." *PRovoke*, PRovoke News and Insights from the Global PR Industry, 29 Apr. 2016, www.provokemedia.com/latest/article/the-cost-of-poor-communications.

## Chapter 8

Fry, Richard. "Millennials Are Largest Generation in the U.S. Labor Force." *Pew Research Center*, Pew Research Center, 27 July 2020, www.pewresearch.org/fact-tank/2018/04/11/millennials-largest-generation-us-labor-force/.